PRACTICAL APPLICATION OF
SCIENCE OF MIND

PRACTICAL APPLICATION OF SCIENCE OF MIND

*by Ernest Holmes
and Willis Kinnear*

SCIENCE OF MIND COMMUNICATIONS
LOS ANGELES, CALIFORNIA

This volume was originally published
as the 1958 Annual Edition of
Science of Mind Magazine.

Eigthteenth Printing — August 1991

*Science of Mind Communications wishes to acknowledge
Mrs. Marion Warfield Hefferlin
through whose generosity this 18th printing was made possible.*

Published by Science of Mind Communications

3251 West Sixth Street, Los Angeles, California 90020

ISBN 0-911336-24-9

CONTENTS

INTRODUCTION

That thought is a continuous creative factor in our everyday living there is no doubt. What we think and the way we feel permeate everything we do and all that we are. The creativity of our thought resides not only in a specifically directed pattern of thinking, but also in the entire content of our body of thought: What do we think about ourselves? our relationship to the world in which we live? our relationship to the unseen creative Power behind the manifest universe?

Recognized or not, in our answers to these questions rests the causes of our experiences in life: our health, our affairs, and our relationships with others. Our belief and conviction about the Reality that exists behind all things should be emotionally acceptable, intellectually sound, and, above all, practical and demonstrable in our lives.

A God that is worshiped on Sunday and promptly forgotten on Monday is not enough. A belief and conviction in a Power greater than we are must be such that it pertains to our every endeavor. The tremendous force and power that is inherent in Life is not a sometime thing, but is in everything at all times. This we need to become convinced of, and our conviction must be brought down to earth. And the application of our conviction in daily living is the most practical and important thing we could ever undertake.

It is the purpose of this book to assist you in establishing and clarifying in your own mind a healthful and sound approach to that spiritual Reality which does exist in the universe and is what you really are. The creativity which resides in the Creator of all things, also resides in your own mind. Your scientific use of it in the Science of Mind is the most valuable thing you can ever learn.

It is easy to show or tell another how to do something, but the actual *doing* each must learn for himself. It is hoped that the various ideas presented here will enable the reader to learn a more practical application of the Science of Mind for a fuller enjoyment of daily living.

ERNEST HOLMES

CHAPTER I

A BASIS FOR THE CREATIVITY
OF THOUGHT

It seems scarcely necessary to say that there is an active spirit of inquiry abroad in the world today. People everywhere are searching for spiritual truth, perhaps as never before in the history of man. The remarkable feature of this search, however, is that not only the average man, but also the scientist in the laboratory, is probing deep into the universe trying to find the source of his being.

There is a definitely growing recognition of the fact that the Universe shows two aspects of activity. We first find that the physical world operates in accord with well-recognized and in-variable laws, apparently without any volition on their part. Then we discover that the directive factor is Conscious Intelligence. These two forms of activity, which may seem to be contradictory to one another, have given rise to different types of thinking. There are those who maintain that man is fixed in a treadmill of life in which he is subject to the blind working of unchangeable law, and that he has very little if anything to say about the matter. Then there are those who ignore or minimize the working of law and say man struggles along through life entirely by a process of "trial and error" and happenstance. It is possible to reconcile these two apparently conflicting views because when seen in their true relation to one another they will be found to be complementary, not antagonistic.

Unquestionably *thought is power*. It is not a vague unpre-dictable influence floating around in the universe. Properly understood, thought is subject to laws as exact as those of chemistry or any other physical science. But at the same time within a law *the individual has the fullest freedom.*

MAN LIVES — AND HE IS A THINKER

There are two observable facts of which we can be certain. The first is that we live; it is impossible for a sane man to doubt the reality of his own existence. The second fact is that we live in a physical world. We experience it every time we bump our heads on something.

A logical question would be: What is it in us that knows these two facts? It certainly is not the brain, which can be similar to an electronic machine. Therefore, there must be something in us that uses the brain to interpret the world about us, that conceives ideas, that reasons concerning life and determines which activities shall follow which conclusions. That something is the real "self." The brain is the physical organ through which the *thinker* thinks, through which Mind functions. Man in his true *inner* self is the Thinker.

NATURAL FORCES ARE NOT CONSCIOUS

It is also observable that the forces of nature do not think, although their action is intelligent and logical. The whole system of science is based upon this factual observation. The action of steam, gravitation, electricity, and every other force in nature, is strictly according to *law.* If there were no invariable law by which they operate there could be no science, because the shifting bases would render it impossible to count on anything. There would be nothing in the world that would work twice in the same way. No one has the power to alter, even in the slightest degree, the laws that control the universe.

We have, therefore, two manifestations of activity: the movement of thought, which is the conscious activity of the mind of man; and the movement of natural physical energy in accord with law, evidenced by an exact mathematical sequence of cause and effect. When we are able to reconcile these two modes of action, we can understand why life is what it is, and better still, we can make life what we wish it to be. So we seek to learn the nature of matter, and of mind.

THE NATURE OF MATTER

Every material object in the universe is composed of certain units called atoms, or "elements," and there are over one hundred of them known. The atoms of hydrogen and oxygen, when combined in a ratio of two to one, become water. All "matter" consists of different groupings of the various atoms. Man's physical body is composed of many of the same type of atoms found in the earth, and even in the stars. In his body they are in different combinations and arrangements.

Any observable mass of matter is large compared to the molecules of which it is composed. When matter is broken down it resolves itself into molecules and they in turn can be resolved into atoms. Going even further, an atom is huge compared with the particles of which it is composed. These infinitesimal particles include the better known nucleus and the electrons about it.

An atom is like a miniature solar system. There is the "nuclear sun" at the center, with electrons whirling at almost unbelievable speed around this center. An idea of the sizes and distances involved in matter may be gained by considering the illustration used by physicists, that if a drop of water were enlarged to the size of the earth, one of the atoms in it would be as large as a baseball. Then if we could think of this atom as being as large as the Empire State Building, its electrons would be as small as the heads of pins. Furthermore, in proportion to the size of the electrons, the distance of their orbits from the nucleus is as great as the distance of the orbit of the earth from the sun.

If this is not too staggering for us to think of, it might be well to go on and ask, "What are electrons made of?"

Electrons are infinitesimal particles of electrical energy, hence their name. The central nucleus, or sun, is positively charged, while the revolving electrons are negatively charged. Matter therefore appears to be a highly concentrated form of electricity. It might be said that the atom, with its nucleus and electrons, the ultimate basis of matter, is energy condensed in its *most* tangible form, and that it is at the same time matter in its *least* tangible form. In other words, in the atom we see energy becoming matter.

Science has shown that every kind of atom is a concretion of energy; thus there must be one fundamental energy which is present everywhere in the universe and which occupies all space, and from which all physical things are made. The nature of a particular atom is determined by the number of its electrons and the charge or size of the nucleus. Truly, the entire physical universe is a unity.

THE NATURE OF THE THINKER

Just as we have found that all matter has a common source, so we also are able to determine that there is One Mind common to all men. The Mind that governs the tiny planetary systems of the atoms that comprise matter is also the mind that is within us.

The force that moves our body is the power of *thought,* and the intelligence that is back of our thought is the Intelligence that runs the universe. Matter, in itself, possesses no power of thought or of independent action, but it is motivated by Consciousness through Law, with the result that it moves as the thought moves.

The infinite Thinker is always thinking perfectly. Its action in man, Its intelligence or thought, must flow through the mental states of man. Man's pattern of thinking is the mold through which Universal Mind flows into manifestation in his experience. We might liken this action to the sea of air about us which we force into balloons of varying sizes, shapes, and colors. It is still the same air, but through man's power of selection he can fill any shaped balloon he wishes. So man can also permit the creativity of the Universe to flow into a mold of his own twisted, distorted thought, and by the same law that would manifest perfection in accord with a perfect mental mold, it will manifest distortion in accord with his distorted mental state.

Thus we may understand why it is that material forms must be manifestations of some pattern of thought. They are Mind in visible form. The physical universe around us, of course, is not created by our individual thought. It is created by the thought of God, or the Universal Thinker; but since the Mind of God is also the mind of man, or the mind *in* man, it follows that man's use of the One Mind individualizes Its creative power in a personal way. A man's body, business, or material possessions are spiritual Energy or Essence become tangible in a form which is a thing of thought.

OUR LIMITING THOUGHT PATTERNS

Since the whole race has believed in limitation throughout the ages, it follows that the limitation created by the race thought operates through all of us to a very large degree. Whether we choose to call it race thought, the human mind, the carnal mind, or collective unconscious, makes no difference. It is probable that the sum total of human thought binds the average individual until he consciously frees himself from it by seeing through it, by knowing it for exactly what it is.

Hell is real enough to the ones who believe in it, but when we transpose a thought of hell to a contemplation of heaven, its supposed flames are at once extinguished. Lack and limitation are real enough in our experience; but if we can push our thought away from them and visualize and accept a greater abundance, having faith that it will appear, then we shall discover that our previous acceptance of the race thought about limitation merely held circumstances in a certain limited form.

The creative Power which we use in doing this is the same Power that creates everything, and since It has no limitation of Itself, and could have none, the only limitation which It has for us is the one we give to It.

This knowledge is a source of great encouragement. For when a man understands it he knows that "what thought has done, thought can undo." He has come to the place where he is able to reconcile the ideas of a world of immutable Law, and of freedom of thought. He lives in a universe pervaded by perfect Intelligence and operating through a perfect Law. At the same time he possesses freedom to choose his own thoughts — create his own thought patterns or forms — in accord with the infinite Perfection, knowing that through Its action as Law they will become physically manifest in his body and his environment. If there is any mystery of life he can know that it is a "sweet mystery" and he can be glad that he has found it.

REMOVE NEGATIVE IDEAS

Man can always change his negative mental states. Just as he can thrust a pin into a balloon and release its enclosed air, so he can eliminate any pattern of thought which may be the cause of any undesirable experience. But in doing this he must separate his action from his emotional reactions which are the result of a lifetime of living; they are habitual, and clamor for control.

It is up to the individual to put negative *feelings* in their proper place, recognize them for what they really are, and proceed to affirm the nature of the Spirit within him. He should recognize that his "feelings" are under the direction of his conscious thought and when they seek to flow back into old negative forms he will assert dominion over them. Then he will approach a problem with eyes open and know there is a solution.

Our thought patterns, being largely habitual, tend to perpetuate themselves. The happy thing to remember is that these thought patterns are always subject to change. Even though they may be in the subconscious part of thought, the subconscious may always be changed by conscious intention. Old undesirable thought patterns may be brought to the surface and their power to perpetuate themselves removed by the very act of knowing that they no longer have power.

It is necessary that we understand this, and it may help us to know that all psychoanalytical processes are conducted on this principle: Thought patterns can be brought to the surface and by being consciously known their negative power becomes dissipated. In psychology this is called "catharsis" and "conversion." A similar process takes place in our use of the Science of Mind as we seek to realize that lack, limitation, fear, doubt, sickness, and pain could not be intended by God. They are merely the misuse of our good. We must convert our old thought patterns into new and better ones.

This is the purpose of meditation, contemplation, and spiritual mind treatment: to change our patterns of thought so that they conform to the greatest possible good, reflecting the nature of the Universe which can only be good. Our every thought is creative in our experience through the creative action of the Law of Mind upon it, so in changing our pattern of thought we do not change the nature of the Law but provide It with a new plan of action. And regardless of what our experience may have been our new thought pattern is what counts now. We are not fighting anything, any idea of the devil, evil, or limitation. We are merely using our God-given right to choose the way we desire to think and through the natural normal creative action of our thought have it become manifest as our tangible experience.

CHAPTER II

TIME FOR A CHANGE

It is a matter of common knowledge and observation that nothing in life can ever remain static — stand still. In considering our affairs, our health, or our relationships there is always a progression or retrogression, a bettering or a worsening of the situation. There is a dynamic Principle of growth and development in the Universe which continually seeks greater expression. Whenever this purposeful activity is hindered, denied, or suppressed, stagnation and deterioration set in. Nature's edict appears to be: *grow and progress* or regress.

One thing that needs always to be kept in mind is the fact that any growth and development involves *change*. There must always be a continual change in all of our situations, there is no standing still in any respect.

A simple illustration is provided by a seed. Once placed in the soil the progression of growth involves swelling up, bursting its shell, and sending forth roots and shoots. The roots probe deeper into the soil and the shoots make their way to the surface and emerge into the sunlight. Changes continue to take place; the plant still grows and develops. The shoot becomes a stalk bearing branches and leaves, which in turn produce flowers and seeds. Every living thing evidences the same dynamic quality of purposeful progression which is founded in continual change.

SOMETHING NEW

In man we find the same activity. Two cells unite and subsequently divide into four, the four into eight, and through the purposeful action of Life we finally find man fully developed with a body comprised of billions of cells, each serving a particular purpose and function. But all of this could not have come about unless there had been changes, each forward step being based on a change for the better from a previous step. And all of this growth and change is carried on through the action of God — infinite Mind — functioning as intelligent Law.

But over and above the purely physical aspect of the growth and development of all living things, something new and different makes its appearance in man. In the human there is an additional channel for growth and increase — self-consciousness. Hence we discover in the function of mind, in the creative activity of thought, a continual urge to create and express.

Our activity of thought is actually a Divine compulsion of the One Mind in us seeking an ever-increasing achievement and expression through us. The forms and outlets for this self-conscious process of thought, which appears as a unique creation of Life in man, may manifest in many ways.

We each interpret and use the urge for greater expression. For some the fulfillment of this inner drive may be found in a new home, a larger pay check, increased business activity, better health, as well as an increasing desire for a greater spiritual awareness. All of these are urges of the indwelling Intelligence which we must either combat and choke down, or to which we must give expression. We cannot stand still. We have to continue to express this action of Life within us because, if we deny ourselves of this activity, we deny ourselves of Life's creativity in every aspect of our experience.

THE CHANGING SCENE

Our lives and experiences may very well be likened to a river. If we stand on the bank of a river and watch it flow by we become aware of the fact that the river never changes but that its content is always new. By analogy we might say the purposeful dynamic quality of Life within us never changes but the content of our experience of living never remains the same.

Our physical body is never the same from one moment to the next. It is constantly in a state of flux. New substance is being added, old discarded. The body is forever remaking itself. The pattern that is followed in this continual remaking may be either one of improved health or poorer health. Our state of health is either being increased or decreased. The pattern of health which is being followed is created by the nature and content of what we think.

The same process also applies to business activities. No individual's or company's financial condition is the same from one moment to the next. Either the profits are greater or the losses are increasing. Even though the cash register may not have rung for an hour the situation has changed. The rent has gone on, salaries are being paid, the light bill has increased — expenses continue. But when sales are made changes occur in the other direction, and according to the dictum that nothing can stand still, that change is constant, we find that the change has been made in a favorable direction.

This brings us to the point where we find ourselves faced with the fact that there must always be changes. The thing that we must ever be aware of is the direction in which change is reflected in our experience. Is it for better or worse? Things are going to change, it is futile to resent or combat them, so it is of prime importance to determine that the changes are in the right direction.

DIRECTING CHANGES

There are not several "laws" as some may think, but only One Law, although It appears in many forms. So regardless of what the change may be, or what it relates to, we find that that which controls it or determines the nature of the change is through the functioning of the One Law.

It was a concept of One Law that led Einstein to develop his Unified Field theory. He felt that the three great physical forces of gravity, magnetism, and electricity of necessity had to be related and could be expressed in terms of one law. His work is being carried on by many brilliant scientists, and one of them, Werner Heisenberg, recently announced that he had achieved Einstein's goal of relating these forces — one formula explaining all three actions.

So similarly we may find that even though all of our experiences, and the changes involved, appear to adhere to many different laws, fundamentally they are all resolvable into One Law. And that Law is the Law of God, Mind, infinite Intelligence — the way and the channel through which It creates, the means by which thought in the Mind of God becomes manifest and expressed. And that which becomes manifest is in accord with the nature of thought. So in the same way we find that the changes which occur in our own personal experiences are manifestations of the creativity of the content of our thought, our conscious or unconscious use of the One Law.

The changes that occur in our experience are directed, are reflections of the pattern of our thinking!

THE RIGHT CHANGES

Just as everything that God creates brings forth "according to its own kind," so we sometimes unhappily discover that our thinking has brought forth in our experience situations which are a reflection of negative or morbid thoughts.

Not only do we find that change is a necessary *must* in living, we also come to realize that a change in our way of thinking is also a *must* if we would have a richer, fuller, more enjoyable life. Our thinking has to change to the affirmative if we would have favorable changes in our experience.

We need to learn to affirm only the things we desire, not what we do not want. We need to think on these things: Life is good, not against us; health is normal and the natural state of our bodies; God always succeeds, and so should we; the Universe is abundant in all good things, and so should be our lives.

It is only through the affirming and the accepting of these things in our pattern of thinking that they may become our experience. Jesus said that a thornbush could not produce grapes or a thistle produce figs. A cat cannot give birth to a dog, nor can a cow produce a kitten. Neither can thoughts of hate create a life filled with love, nor thoughts of limitation provide a life of plenty. The creative nature of our thought is no exception to the lawful activity of the Universe which makes every result correspond to that which initiates the action.

Consequently we find that it is not difficult to understand why the person whose mind is filled with thoughts and fears of illness is the one who is always sick; or the person who is continually bemoaning his poor financial condition always finds himself broke. We can go through the whole category of human activity and we will find the same relationship of thought and experience. And all of this not because of or through any perverse or malicious intent on the part of God or Life, but merely because we have used the Law to bring about undesirable rather than favorable changes. The cause rests not in the nature of the Law, which has no volition, but in the way we have used and directed Its action by the way we think!

In many, many respects we discover that we have to completely reverse our way of thinking.

THE CHOICE IS OURS

We can keep on thinking in negative ways as we have been doing in the past and suffer the results, or since we have the right and the ability to choose we can choose a better pattern of thinking. There is no necessity that we continue to think in any particular way other than our own determination to do so. We can change our thought any time we desire. Ours is the responsibility and obligation to choose and choose wisely. We always hold on to the steering wheel of our thought-life, and through it our experience in life. Our path may be rough or smooth depending on how well we guide and control our thought content. How well do we determine what is worthy or unworthy, desirable or undesirable? How selective are we? Not nearly enough. The power of choice with which man has been endowed is either his greatest blessing or his greatest curse. Properly understood, it can lift him to the heights; misunderstood, it can drag him to the depths. He is free to choose anything which he wishes, but he must accept the responsibility for his choices, because inexorable Law will create his experiences according to his choices.

Some years ago a man tried to do an unfair, unkind thing. He and his wife were separated; he was turning her out to get along as best she could. She had moved into a miserable room with her three young children. The divorce laws of the particular state in which they lived were written in such a way that he could be cruel and unfair if he wished. Friends tried to persuade the man to do the right thing. He was adamant. He set his mouth in a straight line and shouted, "Let them starve. I'll make her dance to my tune, or else."

He had the power to select, and he had selected. What he did not know was that *whatever he would select he would become.* Or we could put it in another way: His thought was creating *his* experience. He went on his way, clinging to this consuming thought of hate until it literally tore him to pieces. His body could not withstand the destructive action of hate. *His own power of selection had been used to destroy himself.*

Quite the reverse is true when one uses his power of selection in a constructive way. When Jesus healed the sick he *consciously selected* the thought of Divine Perfection. Surrounded as he was by the complaints, the cries, the many forms of sickness in others, he withdrew within his own consciousness and there deliberately contacted the Divine Perfection.

He resolutely closed his mind to the apparent imperfection all about him. *He saw God, the All-Good.* The result of this selection raised his level of thought to the Divine level. He saw and knew nothing of disease — he consciously knew Spirit as unsick, whole, vital, harmonious.

Since thoughts are things, his idea of God was manifest in a way that was the very opposite of what happened in the life of the man who carried hate in his heart. It took the shattered, paralyzed body of the man who lay at the Pool of Siloam and the constructive change was wrought so that he arose, took up his bed, and walked.

The Law manifests for us that which we have mentally accepted, and does it in an entirely neutral, impersonal way. It does not try to punish the one man and love the other. It knows only to do, and cares not about that which It does.

CHANGE FOR THE BETTER

There are going to be changes in our lives from hour to hour and day to day, and we cannot escape them. It is the nature of the Universe. Let us accept change, make the most of it, and capitalize on it. The action of the Law never changes, but the direction of the action is always up to us. Life can become a glorious adventure, increasingly filled with more of every good thing as we gradually or suddenly come to change our pattern of thinking so that it embraces more of those good things.

Life can become fun, an experience of continual expectancy. For as we change our thought today we can change the undesirable aspects of our health, relationships, and affairs into ones more to our liking tomorrow.

We are going to change, and that is wonderful for who would want things to stay eternally the same regardless of what they are. We would soon become so bored and fed up that we would lose all desire to live. We should be eager for change, look forward to it, but let us be sure the change is for the better. And this we can do with ease by the simple process of maintaining our pattern of thought in conformity with what we know the nature of God must be — the ultimate Good in and as all things.

CHAPTER III

BUSINESS CAN BE GOOD

The Science of Mind can be applied to every department of man's activity. People sometimes say that while they can see how the mind can control the body and its states of health, they cannot feel the same confidence in regard to business, the sale of property, profit in investments, and such financial activities as are common to our economic setup. This is a false notion which must be replaced by the certainty that Mind operates in everything that goes on in the universe.

The error, in many instances, is due to carrying over certain concepts from restricted religious thinking. The older theology taught that God singled out one man and poured into his life great riches, honor, fame, and what is known as "success." Toward another man God often adopted a different attitude. He withheld these things for some reason which man could not fathom. This man probably worked as hard, was as sincere and honest, yet things continually went wrong. Just at the time when he had struggled out from under a load of debt and could see daylight ahead, some unforeseen sickness, with its attendant hospital or doctor's bills, would come along and fling him back under the load once more. If he managed to battle his way out of this situation, the next upset would be that he would lose his job. If he managed to save a little money and invest it, the investment would fail.

Ignorant of the Law of Mind, many have had no other answer to this tragic situation than that "God willed it so," and that man's duty in this event was to resign himself to the will of God, accept his hard lot, and try to "grow spiritually."

Years of thinking along any one line will leave their mark, and one of the things we must do is to divorce our present thinking from any of our old ideas which tend toward limitation. God's Nature could only be that there is for us an ever-increasing demonstration and experience of the good things of life. Health is just as material an activity as money-making; and if God-Mind can be called in to promote a man's health, It can just as truly and confidently be trusted to promote his bank account.

PROPERTY IS SPIRITUAL

Recently a man came in for assistance. He had saved his money and bought a small apartment building. He had figured the income which the rentals would bring in, deducted the interest, taxes, and other expenditures which would be necessary, and after allowing for an occasional vacancy he still had anticipated a nice living for himself.

But after acquiring ownership things turned out other than he had planned. The place was very difficult to rent. Tenants moved out and few came in response to his advertising. He spent even larger sums for advertisements. Still the renters stayed away. It looked as if he would lose the property. He said, "When I leave you today I wish I didn't have to go back to the deadness of the place; I have come to *hate* the very sight of it."

During the conversation it developed that he doubted very much if God cared whether he rented the place or not. "I have tried to believe it," he said, "but I cannot pray with assurance, because after all, for some hidden reason, God might want me to lose the property."

It was called to his attention that there must first of all be a clear understanding of the spiritual nature of property. The earth was an earlier manifestation of God than man was. The earth was formed as the abode of coming man, and was so constructed as to provide him with sustenance. This part of the creation of God is as spiritual as any other, and must be so understood. When it was brought into form it was good. Anything that God makes is good.

COWORKERS WITH GOD

There must be the realization that we are coworkers with God. We are dealing with the formed earth, which we recognize as the creation of God, and we are One with God in our mastery of the earth. Everything in the Universe is harmoniously existing for the good of every other part, so the earth certainly is not withholding its cooperation. We tell it to bring forth substance for us, as the farmer sows so he may reap. Sustenance might be in the form of crops, or it might be in the form of buildings. If our livelihood is through rentals or the sale of property we have as much right to expect success as the farmer does. Therefore, we work together with God to make this property produce a living — a good crop of rentals.

Another thing that he was told was that he must substitute love for hate. He had come to hate the property, the creation of God. We mentally separate ourselves from anything we hate, therefore, he was separating himself from his good through his feeling against the apartments. It was suggested that he tell the property how much he loved it, and that he take the necessary time to induce within himself this deep-seated love for the property, not necessarily as a bringer of income, but first and foremost as a part of God's creation.

It was explained to him that there must be an acceptance of the fact that the Law of Mind works as readily in this circumstance as It does in the matter of physical healing. That the people who need these apartments, want them, like them, and have the money to pay for them, can be his tenants. He must love these people before he sees them and know that they will enjoy living in this particular place. If the thought arises, "It is a poor renting locality," he must immediately substitute the conviction, "This is a good locality, very desirable for those whom Mind brings to it. They like it for special reasons which are not recognized by others who pass it by. God knows it to be good and I affirm that it is good."

SEE THE DEAL COMPLETED

Just as he was able to look backward, by calling upon memory, and bring people and incidents out of the past into the present, so he had to be able to envision the way things could become. Instead of thinking, "Oh, I hope I can persuade someone. I'll promise him anything to get him in. I'll cut the rent or make other concessions because he may be the only one who looks at it," the attitude should be, "This place has a value, is fairly priced, and is exactly what is wanted by the one to whom Mind already has rented it." He must know that "the property is rented in Mind at this moment. Mind knows no past, no future, only the now. Therefore, this good is complete. It is here now. Mind has rented these apartments now to people I have not yet met, but I give thanks for this accomplished fact. They are living happily now in these apartments. The very people whom I shall yet see in the flesh, are there now in Mind. I rejoice and give thanks for this and for them."

As he induced this inward conviction that the place was already rented, a change came in his mental state. He no longer worried over the question, "Will this be rented?" Rather it was, "I know it is rented. If one person does not take it, then I know that he is not the one; and instead of being depressed and discouraged I look expectantly toward the coming of the right one, knowing that he surely is coming to inquire, see the apartment, like it, and take it, paying a fair rent for it."

This is what Jesus tried to impress on us when he said to those who were tensed and strained by their fears that they would not have enough to eat, drink, or wear: "Seek ye first the kingdom [inner awareness] of God, and his righteousness [righteousness]; and all these things shall be added unto you." *Always look beyond the channel to the Source.*

The next day five men moved in. They were from a construction crew that was to start digging a flood-control channel in the neighborhood. They moved their families into all but one of the vacant apartments. Three days later an elderly couple from the East moved in, and the eight apartments were filled.

The ditch-digging job ended at about the same time that the Easterners left for their home. At this time a trucking and contracting company moved its business into the neighborhood. The drivers and helpers rented apartments, and the owner learned that God's Nature is not limitation, but full and complete expression. He learned that Mind operates in the field of finance just as surely as in that of health.

THE MATERIAL AND THE SPIRITUAL ARE ONE

The same underlying philosophy operates in all fields of business. Property, goods, and services may have all the appearance of materiality, yet to him who understands the spiritual and mental nature of the Universe they are spiritual and mental. Too many persons interested in metaphysics separate things into spiritual and material. Most property owners think in terms of material, such as size and location of the lot, the physical type and quality of the buildings, nearness to transportation, measured earning power, the fact that more modern property is nearby.

In our use of the Science of Mind we do not throw these proved fundamentals of business to one side. We study all of them, recognize them, and are very careful to have our investments conform to the rules of good business. Yet we realize that the control of the situation is mental and spiritual. We recognize nothing in the material world that can hinder the free flow of Mind in and through our business, and we thereby invest our undertaking with something more than the mere physical basis upon which a bank would loan money— that is, facts and figures which can be set down and analyzed on paper. We add to the undertaking a spiritual quality that is more real than all the balance sheets, such as the right action which led people to live in the above mentioned apartments, meeting the needs of both the tenants and the owner.

WHY SOME BUSINESSES SUCCEED

Some businesses possess that certain something which draws success to them. That something is the inner consciousness of the owner or management. All business success is in the inner consciousness of those in charge. Business never grows by accident or "luck." A person who knows, and knows that he knows, who has a proper understanding of the spiritual nature of money and builds it into his inner consciousness, will have a better business than he who does not.

The salesman who applies this principle which we have been discussing will sell more goods. He cannot fail to do so. Having selected a line of goods to sell — a line which has merit, which is fairly priced, not necessarily the cheapest, and which fills a need in society — he can, using honest, sincere methods of merchandising, sell very profitable quantities of his product through good and so-called bad times, as long as he keeps "bad times" out of his own consciousness.

When one knows deeply within himself that there is only One Mind; that the mind of his prospect, his own mind, and Universal Mind are One; when he knows that his goods are nothing less than Mind in tangible form; when he recognizes that the amount of his sales are determined within himself, and that he first forms these sales as a mental concept within his own consciousness; that as they are firmly established in Mind they will assuredly take form because they *are* Mind in form; when one knows this then his sales will mount.

WE CONTRIBUTE TO THE SOCIAL ORDER

Each of us has a distinct individuality, we have different abilities and capabilities. Each, because of these differences, reflected in temperament and mental outlook, has something unique to contribute to mankind. Never waste time envying that which the other fellow seems to have. Each has something that the other does not have. If all people had what the other fellow has it would have no value in the world because there would be no one to whom it would be a contribution.

Each in his own particular way is fulfilling the purpose of the Life that is within him. As we make our individual contribution to the social order we are fulfilling the expression of Life in us and we can be sure that others will contribute to our good. In accordance with the Law of Cause and Effect we have every right to expect that our contribution will in turn draw to us ample supply, high success, and an ever-increasing expression of good. Only one person in the entire universe can hinder an individual from accomplishing this, and that person is himself.

Since the individual himself is the only one who can hinder the desired result from taking place in his experience, then it naturally follows that success also resides in the nature of his own thought. This is one of the all-important points in our demonstrating the Science of Mind through spiritual mind treatment. It means that *all treatment is self-treatment*. If the Spirit is already willing, and if the Law must obey, it logically follows that the demonstration must first take place in the mind of the one giving the treatment, whether he is working for himself or someone else.

It is indeed fortunate that this is so, else we should all be compelled to admit our destiny lies outside ourselves. Unless there were a Power within us which, consciously used, produces definite results, then there would be no Science of Mind and no spiritual universe available for our use. Whoever said, "Be still and know that I am God," must have perceived this. All treatment is self-treatment, and so far as we are concerned, in using this Law we shall never have anyone to convince but ourselves.

How necessary it is, then, that we become fully convinced not only of the Divine Presence, but of the supremacy of the Law! The way successfully to give a spiritual mind treatment is to *work with our own thought until we, ourselves, believe what we have stated. This may take one moment, one hour, one day, one week, one month, one year — no one can answer this problem for us but ourselves.* What we are merges with the great Reality of the universe and is One with the only Power in the universe. But we must consciously use this Power if we expect definite results. Again, Power unused will do nothing. We must *recognize* spiritual Power, and then *use* It.

CHAPTER IV

HOW IS YOUR HEALTH?

Many people who can answer all the questions asked about the mechanics of healing through spiritual mind treatment fail to receive help because they are unwilling to pay the price. This price often involves the giving up of some weakness, a negative pet emotional mood, or patterns of thinking, and the cultivating of an opposite and positive attitude.

When Jesus said, " . . . sin no more, lest a worse thing come unto thee," he was not threatening or using an appeal to fear. Sin means making a mistake or missing the mark. There is no sin but a mistake and no punishment but a consequence. So when Jesus said, "sin no more," he was not hurling theological invective; he was merely pointing to the Law of Cause and Effect. It stands to reason if certain mental attitudes have produced certain conditions, then a continuation of such attitudes will perpetuate such conditions. There must always be soul-searching to find whether or not we are living in accord with the Law of Good. One thing is certain: We cannot fool the Universe. This is what true spiritual understanding does for the individual, it sets him back on the right track, always pointing to the great Reality which harmoniously governs everything.

HEALING COMES FROM UNITY

Once a person has grasped the idea that healing follows in such degree as he has realized his Oneness with God, he is very likely to ask, "And just how far does this Oneness with God extend?" The answer is, "In our experience it extends just as far as we allow it." When we understand this Oneness we can realize that the more closely our thoughts and actions coincide with the Divine Nature the more perfectly we experience It, and the more perfectly we experience It the more effectively we shall be able to constructively use the creative Law of Mind. Thus, as we open our lives to the inflow of Divine healing Power we also release more of everything God-like *through* us.

Just as we should recognize our Oneness with the Source of health so should we recognize our Oneness with the Source of love. There is only One Health in the entire universe; we enjoy this when we identify ourselves intimately with It. There is only One Love in the universe, and we experience It by identifying ourselves with It. Since there is only One Mind in the entire universe we experience more of It when we become aware that our mind is an individualization of It. There is only One Mind — the Mind of God — full of Life and Intelligence for all. This Life is overflowing with creative and healing action, therefore as we consciously become one with It we enter into an experience that is normal and healthy, untroubled, and at peace.

NO ROOM FOR HATREDS

As we enter into a sense of Unity with Life and all the good that flows from It we shall find less and less room for hatred, bitterness, criticism, and envy. We shall open our inner lives to the perfect, free, unhindered inflow of Divine Love. Thus we pass from an incomplete experience of life into a life that is God-like. We raise our consciousness to a higher level — a level where there is a consuming desire to do good to others, and where lesser desires gradually fade out. There shall be no room for personal enmities. If there has been an enemy we freely forgive him, for *hatred and healing* can never abide in the same consciousness, nor in the same body.

It is at this very point where many healings are obstructed. We want our "blessing" but we also want to retain a pet bitterness toward someone else. In a sense this retention of a bitter feeling is a subjective desire to shut them off from a blessing similar to that which we desire to receive, and in mentally shutting them off we unknowingly shut ourselves off.

The person who holds a grudge bars himself from the highest expression of his Divine nature. God never hates, nor does He hold feelings of bitterness toward any person. Thus the grudge-holder is trying to express God and something else, which is impossible. God is not cut up into little sections. No one can say, "I will accept His healing but not express His love." Since God is indivisible, the person who refrains from expressing His Love finds himself unable to accept His Health. Therefore, we should express Love, for Love is the fulfilling of the Law.

FORGIVE, RIGHT NOW

The one who is spiritually aware of his Oneness with God freely forgives everyone with whom he has ever had a difference. He does not wait until he feels himself to be in a forgiving mood. He does not even wait to separate the sheep from the goats, and say, "This one I can freely forgive, but this other one is too mean, so I'll reserve a little private hatred for him." No, he encompasses all in a sense of love, without waiting to ask if they are deserving or not. This does not mean that we must accept everyone's opinion about us or that we must agree with those ideas which we feel are contradictory to an intelligent outlook on life. It merely means that we maintain a good-natured approach in our relationship with people.

Here is a good affirmation to use in this regard: "I bless and love everything that God has created. He sees Himself in His handiwork, and so do I. I refuse to see anything but good in anyone. I now look for and find the good in all men, even those who may have hurt me."

In spiritual mind treatment we must separate our thought about the *real* person from our thought about what ails the physical or psychological man. The *real* man is always spiritual and perfect. It is the psychological and physiological man who needs to be healed. We may have sympathy with a person without sympathizing with his troubles. We can enter into a consciousness of love for his spiritual nature without entering into a consciousness of unity with either his psychological or physiological discord.

For instance, if we are treating ourselves or someone who has had a great deal of discord or hate in his life, we must rise above both the psychological reaction to life and the physiological correspondent. We must cause our own consciousness to rise in love and appreciation for man's *real* nature to a point where this knowing removes all ideas of hate, and this knowing also eliminates all other discord. Any denials and affirmations which we make in such a spiritual mind treatment, which are a true appreciation of man's *real* nature, are for the purpose of *clarifying our own thought;* the removing of any obstructions from it which deny us the ability to rise above the discord and the confusion to the place where our affirmation becomes a more complete declaration of Divine Harmony.

WE DON'T CONDEMN

There is no personal God who withdraws His favors from a person as we might from a stubborn child who refuses to cooperate. There is no such thing as punishment *for* sin. We are punished *by* our sins, but never *for* them. Every action, every thought that we think, carries within itself its own consequence, for good or ill. Every act is tied inseparably to its own result, and a man can no more get away from the consequences of his thoughts than he can get away from his own shadow.

It has been truly said that the spiritual confessional is the greatest psychiatrist on earth. Jesus sometimes forgave people their sins before he healed them. Some psychologists tell us that there is a secret sense of guilt back of every neurosis. If so, how important it is that we should seek to remove the pressure of every sense of guilt from our own thinking. In a correct use of the Science of Mind we need to know that God holds nothing against anyone, and that Divine forgivingness is a necessary complement to Divine givingness. Any sense of guilt which we have, any burden of condemnation which we entertain, or any mental state which weighs us down, hinders us from more fully experiencing the nature of spiritual Reality.

We need to remove any such obstructions. We need to know that sin is a result of ignorance; to know that Spirit never holds anything against us. But also we must never forget that since the Law of Cause and Effect is always working, punishment will always follow wrongdoing. It is impossible for a person to undertake a series of spiritual mind treatments without arriving at a more clarified spiritual awareness in his thought. He not only will be less likely to make mistakes, but he will also have less desire to engage in any destructive act or thought.

WHAT ABOUT MEDICAL ASSISTANCE?

Some schools of metaphysical thought believe that it is wrong to seek medical assistance under any circumstances. And while we hold no controversy over this subject, it is entirely fitting that we make our position clear. The Science of Mind has no superstitions, holds to no dogmas, but believes in the good in everything. We sincerely believe that any undesirable physical condition can be bettered through the proper use of prayer, faith, or spiritual affirmation. We are equally certain that not all people who have asked for such help have finally been healed. If one is able to say to a paralyzed man, "Take up your bed and walk," and have the man actually take up his bed and walk, then there is certainly no point left to argue over. But what right have we to deny anyone whatever help he can find?

Possibly someone will ask, "But are you not resorting to material means in order to assist the Spirit?" The answer is, "Not at all." There are no material means so far as Spirit is concerned. Divine Intelligence has conceived and created everything. And everything which God has made must be good if we could only understand its true nature. The mental attitude that one cannot receive spiritual benefit if he is being attended by a physician, seems to us to be built upon superstition. Rather, we believe in the most complete cooperation among all of the healing arts; the complete cooperation between the physician, the psychologist, the metaphysician, and the spiritual counselor.

We know that the ultimate in healing is spiritual healing. This spiritual healing may be a result of earnest prayer, of exalted faith, or of spiritual affirmations. It is useless to quibble over terms. We know that faith and conviction must be arrived at, and it does not seem fruitful to argue over what methods one should use, or to say that one method is right while another is wrong. Any method which is constructive is right, if it finally arrives at the desired goal. Why not combine them all and thereby, happily, enjoy the greatest posssible good.

WHAT HEALS?

The fact that all branches of the healing profession succeed in some healing is an indication that underneath all these healings there must be some contact with a spiritual principle of healing which is universal. As one wise physician said, "I treat the patient, but God heals him." The one who understands this is able to *know* in a spiritual mind treatment that the *real* man is Divinely perfect; that the appearance of disease is no part of the *real* man, and that his body is pure spiritual substance in form. One needs to work with these ideas until he convinces himself that he is a spiritual entity, a living expression of perfect Life, Divinely created, sustained, and maintained. So far as a spiritual mind treatment is concerned, it begins and ends in our own mind. *We do not hold thoughts, we do not suggest, we do not will* anything to happen. What we do is to recognize our spiritual nature, to realize the Divine Perfection in, around, and through us, functioning in every organ of our being. We work with these ideas until in our own mind we realize the spiritual Reality of our being. This is all that we could do, this is all that we need try to do, and if we do this successfully our work will be effective.

In using spiritual mind treatment for better health we should constantly keep ourselves alive to the greatness of the Law of Mind; Its constant action, Its irresistibility, Its thoroughness and Intelligence. We should spend much time in meditation upon our Oneness with the Divine Presence, and in the contemplation of the fact that all men, no matter how apparently ill, are indivisibly one with this same Presence. And never, for one moment, should we allow ourselves to admit even secretly that some diseases are amenable to treatment while others are not. We must persistently *know,* without the slightest equivocation, that each can be helped, no matter what his physical condition may be.

CHAPTER V

HOW TO IMPROVE CONDITIONS

It is only right that we should seek to develop a well-balanced outlook upon life. The very nature of this endeavor and undertaking brings us face to face with a most dynamic concept. For the first time, perhaps, we may sense the tremendous possibility of a life lived in the clear light of reason. For the first time, also, we may become aware of potentialities which are far beyond the experience of the average person.

Naturally, when one affirms that the universe in which we are living is a spiritual system, governed by the Law of Mind, those who have given but little thought to the subject may think he is announcing that one can have whatever he wants, can do exactly as he sees fit, and can dominate and control everything within his reach. Fortunately, however, this is only partly true. There is nothing either unreasonable or irrational about this science; it is intensely sane, practical, and never should be associated with anything weird or queer.

Therefore, if anyone asks the question, "Can I become a millionaire over night simply by affirming that I have a million dollars?" the answer would be that nothing could be further from the truth. There are too many misguided people in dire circumstances who are affirming "I am rich." In a certain sense their affirmation is correct, but frequently they overlook the fundamental premise of the Science of Mind, which is that *Spirit can do for us only that which It does through us.* Too often people make the mistake of *mentally wishing* instead of *intelligently thinking.* Too often they fail to realize that they have a definite part to play in the relationship between God and man.

INTELLIGENT THOUGHT IMPROVES CONDITIONS

It is unquestionably true that the Science of Mind, properly understood and applied, can and does improve one's material conditions. It is likewise true that the one who clearly knows his Oneness with all Supply will incorporate that affirmation into his science of living. But the Science of Mind is certainly not a get-rich-quick scheme that enables one to ignore the laws of the Universe and simply affirm himself into wealth. Man receives more as he grows more, and as he grows he learns more perfectly to apply those principles which underlie all successful action.

Proper understanding of his relationship to the Universe, supported by intelligent, industrious work, will add materially to his measure of success. Work without vision is drudgery, but vision without work is self-deception. The well-balanced man can walk with his head in the clouds and still keep his feet solidly planted on the ground. Faith and work are ineffective when separated.

The man who wishes to demonstrate happiness will never be able to do so while his consciousness remains filled with thoughts of inharmony. If he gives the major portion of his waking hours to dwelling upon thoughts of unhappiness, of the injustice of others toward him, of their unlovable qualities, of the hard row he has to hoe compared with that of others, then he might just as well give up the illusion that he will ever experience peace. But the very moment he deliberately casts out every thought of self-pity, and consciously turns away from the apparent injustices in human experience, then he *has started* upon his demonstration of happiness.

DEMONSTRATING SUPPLY

In like manner one cannot spend his time saturating his consciousness with thoughts of limitation and expect to manifest prosperity. It may be a fact that the bills are not paid, work may be scarce, but in the practical application of the Science of Mind he must learn that the *very first step* toward right action lies in knowing, and if he is to change his outward condition he must first change his inner pattern of thinking. Even when he is explaining to the collector at the door just why he cannot meet that bill today, he must learn to detach himself from the *acceptance* of poverty as a logical or normal state.

This does not mean that he airily dismisses his obligations to others with a wave of his hand. He recognizes their validity, but at the same time he knows that his present straitened circumstances .are the result of a "poverty consciousness," a "times are tough consciousness," and he determines that the future will reflect his new consciousness of abundant supply.

Difficult to do this? Yes, it is, if a pattern of negative thinking has become habitual. But when one is definitely changing from the average man's way of thinking he knows that he must expect to exert a special effort, at first, in changing the context of his thought. The rewards will repay him well for he will find himself moving out of present negative circumstances as surely as the sun rises. As soon as the inner attitude changes, the outer experience will change to conform to it, quickly or slowly according to the measure of his mental acceptance.

FREEDOM IS THE NATURE OF SPIRIT

If the thought arises that all men are not intended to experience freedom from financial worries — that perhaps there is some unrevealed reason why an inscrutable Providence allows or desires us to continue in hardship — then let us remember that it is always the purpose of Life to increase the good which man has rather than to take it away. An illustration from nature may help us at this point.

Nature spurs every living thing on to greater freedom and makes us intolerant of anything that hampers that freedom. The trapped bird often will die within a day in its frantic efforts to escape to freedom. The wild animal paces incessantly up and down, seeking a way of escape from the limiting cage. Tree roots will break through a sidewalk for freedom. The will toward freedom is an instinct in everything that lives.

It may be freedom from domination of an individual, or freedom from poverty, or from criticism, or from the absence of love; but, whatever the reason, it is still an urge for freedom even though it might be mistaken. So is the urge for a nicer home, a better automobile, more sales, a bigger pay check, or a more important job. It is not necessarily a reasoned impulse — it may not even be recognized, and certainly not premeditated — it is inherent in the law of our being. We cannot deny it and be happy.

It is not a sign of greed when one desires to build a bigger business or receive a larger pay check. This is a natural urge, for it is the endeavor of Spirit to multiply Its gifts to us so that It may multiply Its Self-expression through us. It is Its nature to express freedom.

WHEN IS FREEDOM WRONG?

The only time freedom is wrong for us is when it infringes upon the freedom of another. Our freedom ends when it infringes upon another's freedom. Since we can only get the good we desire through the operation of the Law of Life, then that same Law is also the Law of freedom for our neighbor as well as for ourselves.

Dishonesty, fraud, or deliberate infliction of suffering upon others can never be connected with our experiencing a greater good for ourselves. If the thing we want can hurt another, then we are misusing the Law, which can only result in detriment to ourselves.

This should not be misconstrued to mean that we shall never hurt anyone by our decisions. Sometimes other people may seek to keep us from expressing our freedom by the plea that by doing so we shall make them unhappy. As a matter of fact, they are infringing upon our freedom every day that they try to keep us in bondage.

Many a person today is remaining in bondage, stifling the free flow of Spirit through him simply because he is told that his good would rob some selfish person of happiness. Sometimes it is a parent who holds an unmarried son or daughter by pleading with them not to leave home in order to better themselves, or by asking them not to marry because then "Mother would be so lonely." This is selfishness on the part of the parent who has lived his life fully and who now would deny the grown child a natural expression and a normal fulfillment of life.

The child therefore has to make his own decision. Few are willing to appear hardhearted toward parents, so they decide to remain in bondage. What such people should see clearly is that the unhappiness is not caused by their selfishness, but by the other's selfishness which would hold them in violation of a law of Life. It is like the boy who, reproved for pulling the cat's tail, replied that he was not pulling it — that he was only holding it; the cat was doing the pulling.

SEEING OURSELVES IN PERFECTION

We have spoken of the necessity of turning completely away from undesirable conditions and forming new thought patterns by a deliberate choice or selection of ideas embodying the good we desire. We should take time daily to see ourselves as we really want to be — we should see ourselves as living happily in our new circumstances, bringing into our consciousness the particular events or situations in which our happiness or greater good seems to be centered. It may be a happy marriage, a new home, a business of our own, or better business where we are; whatever it is, there should be a quiet unstrained acceptance of the fact that *it is right for us, is possible for us, and already is ours in Mind.*

We should keep our thinking wide open to good, completely receptive to it, and we should surround the idea of good with a real warmth of loving expectation. We should regard it joyously, knowing that it will increase our happiness, never diminish it.

We should never lose sight of the fact that it is our entire mental content that is reflected as our experiences. This is fundamental. True, other factors enter in, such as a common-sense attitude toward money, and our willingness to work industriously, and to do the very best work of which we are capable, whether we work for others or are in business for ourselves. But the determining factor, first and last, is our own thought content which we now know can be changed. We do have the power to remold old patterns of thinking and have them manifest as new conditions about us.

APPROACH THE LAW NATURALLY

We must rid ourselves of any tendency toward superstition regarding the Law of Mind. It is completely impersonal. The Law of Mind moves through every thought, good or bad, and brings it into form as tangible experience. This Law might be termed the impersonal side of Life, and should be approached normally and naturally, as we would approach the soil when planting a seed, knowing that it will receive any seed from anybody and grow it into manifestation.

By the impersonal side of Life is meant the Law of Mind or the Law of Cause and Effect. We have already encountered the idea that Spirit is personal to each one of us — is what we are. But the action of Life in the universe as Law is always impersonal. An understanding of this is most vital and basic to the Science of Mind.

Law is subject to our conscious use. Being impersonal, It does not know who is using It or for what purpose. Law has no personal choice in the matter. Its nature always is to respond to our use of It. When we speak of the impersonal side of Life we are really referring to the whole universe of Law, whether we call such laws physical or metaphysical. Law is intelligent in Its action, always acting through the conscious Intelligence in God and man.

THE BASIS FOR PRAYER

The personal aspect of God, the spiritual essence of Reality, is the Divine Intelligence with which we may commune. By intuition, meditation, and prayer we bring ourselves into a conscious and direct relationship with the Spirit within us—God. This has always been the office of prayer and of spiritual contemplation. It is necessary that we should spend a definite time each day in such communion, seeking a greater awareness of Spirit.

When it comes to using the laws of nature, we are acting in accord with the inspiration which we have drawn from Spirit. We are working with the impersonal side of the Universe, a government of law. How can we expect any law to do anything for us in a definite way unless we first understand how the law works and consciously use it for definite purposes? This is what constitutes the technique of any science.

LAW IS ALWAYS EXACT

Unfortunately, many persons seem to think that in the realm of mind they are not dealing with definite laws of cause and effect. For some peculiar reason they feel law no longer holds true. But such is not the case. The Law of Mind is just as exacting as any other law. It has no specific intention whatsoever relative to the individual life until the individual gives It such intention. But once having received this intention, which is provided by the individual's thought, It can only *respond by correspondence*. In this way, when we turn an idea over to the action of Law, It at once begins to act creatively upon the idea without argument, without delay, and without deviating from the content of the idea which we hand It.

This will explain one of the seeming mysteries surrounding the teachings of the great and the wise of the ages, but which few people have properly analyzed. For instance, Jesus told us that when we ask God for anything we must believe that we already have the thing that we are asking for. This is a veiled statement of the Law of Cause and Effect. It really means that we must have a mental acceptance of our desire before the Law can act upon that desire in an affirmative way.

In giving a spiritual mind treatment for ourselves or for another we are told to accept the thing we desire even before we experience it; for unless we accept it we are rejecting it; and if we are rejecting it we are not believing that we have it; and while we believe that we do not have it the Law cannot make the gift. Hence, we are told to believe that we already possess the object of our desire, and so should make known our requests with thanksgiving. A little thought given to this idea will clearly demonstrate that there is no other way prayer could be answered, there is no other way a demonstration could be made. We have the inspiration, the intuition, the instruction of the wise, the dictates of common sense, and a definite knowledge of the Law of Cause and Effect and how It works in practical experience. From all these sources we draw this one and inevitable conclusion: *When a spiritual mind treatment is given it must incorporate an affirmative acceptance of the fulfillment of the desired good; it must state that we now already have that good.*

CHAPTER VI

FACING FACTS

"Life is what we make it." Of course we do not mean that anything we, as individuals, can do will change the nature of Reality. It is self-evident that we cannot do this. What we can do is to change our individual relationship to Reality so that It presents us with new and happier experiences. This is the practical application of the Science of Mind.

If we wish to "make life our servant instead of our master" we must come to understand what the laws of nature are and comply with them. Since this is true of physical laws, it must equally be true of mental and spiritual laws. We need to understand that they are as definite as any other laws of nature.

ONE INTELLIGENCE

Much of science, philosophy, and religion confirms the fact that infinite Intelligence is the final, absolute, and only creative Power in the universe. In adopting the concept that there is a Principle of Mind we have not departed from what would be considered scientific procedure in any other field of knowledge. Just as it has been established that there is but one ultimate electric energy, so we should assume that there is but one ultimate Mind. Just as electric energy operating through an individual bulb will light a particular space without in any way violating its original nature, so we should assume that in like manner the mind of each individual is some part of a Universal Mind. Or, to state the proposition in another way, there is One Universal Mind which is individualized in each person, and which each may use to a greater or lesser degree.

It is this simple but fundamental fact, basic in the Science of Mind, which differentiates its practice from the field of mental suggestion, will power, mental concentration, or from any endeavor to coerce, control, or force anything.

CREATIVITY

The Universe at Its center is pure Spirit or infinite Knowingness. Spirit creates in accord with the Law of Its own nature — the potentiality of infinite Doingness — and at the same time It is the substance of Its creation. We also assume what the inspired of all ages have proclaimed, that the Divine Reality Itself never changes, although It is forever expressing in infinite variation. This entire concept is backed by every scientific discovery that has yet been made, and, so far as we know, has never had any logical argument or known fact contradict it.

Science knows energy as indestructible and limitless. It appears in tangible form as substance. Nothing is either added to or taken from it. Therefore, we conclude that all change is a play of Life upon Itself. It is an inner movement of the Creative Principle upon Itself, which constitutes Its sole and only activity.

With the inspired of the ages we discover that the Universe consists of pure Spirit which has an irresistible urge toward Self-expression. Spirit's creative action is through Law, which is always a servant. Every initiating cause carries within it the seed of its resulting effect through the Law of Cause and Effect. Man's place in this creative order is to express, on the scale of the indivilual life, the same creative activity which Spirit expresses in the life of the Cosmos.

BONDAGE AND FREEDOM

At first man is ignorant of this, his true nature. Consequently, because of his limited understanding he often binds himself by the very law by which he might just as easily have produced freedom. He has created an apparent duality out of an absolute Unity, and he has suffered the consequences. Ignorance of this truth is our great mistake. Enlightenment is our only salvation;

it comes through the knowledge of man's true relationship to the Infinite — God.

Throughout the ages there have been those who *by intuition* have arrived at these conclusions, and *by faith* have demonstrated the transcendent nature of Reality as It flows through the consciousness of man. As we seek to discover the secret of their wisdom, we come to feel it is nothing more mysterious than a firm conviction that the Invisible responds to man and that man measures out the nature of Its creative action in his experience according to his thought, emotions, imagination, and inner conviction. We also arrive at the conclusion, which we feel is self-evident, that Divine Creativity is consciously available to us only in such degree as we ourselves recognize It and realize we are One with It, One with God. This seems self-evident since the Universe cannot be divided against Itself. Therefore, we are justified in believing that man's use of this creative Power must always be in exact proportion to his recognition of his own unity with Good.

POWER OF THOUGHT

From the creative power of thought, which we all possess, there is no escape. It merely becomes a question of how we shall use it. To state the proposition in the simplest manner: There is an infinite Thinker forever thinking Itself into form; there is an infinite Law forever acting upon thought, and creation is the result. Man is some part of this process. Our thought is creative not because we will it to be so but because this is its nature.

Since the Infinite can never be in opposition to Itself, otherwise It would be self-destructive, Its fundamental nature is beneficence, goodness, truth, and beauty. Only in such degree as the individual embodies this nature does he have any real power. It is also true that if in our thinking, our use of the Law of Cause and Effect, we would seek to cause harm to another or deprive another, it is we ourselves who are deprived or harmed. We feel that history proves this principle to be correct.

If we assume that these ideas are correct, it then follows that whenever any individual, or group of individuals, reverses a negative use of this Law and complies with the infinite Harmony, such a person, or group, must automatically prosper. This opens up for us a practical application of this Principle of Mind, for it is to Its correct use that the world must look for the salvation that it so greatly needs, both individually and collectively.

There is an irresistible Universal and Divine urge within us to be happy, to be whole, and to express the fullness of Life. The latent Divinity within us stirs our imagination and, because of Its insistent demand, impels and compels our growth. It is back of every invention; It proclaims Itself through every creative endeavor; It has produced sages, saints, and saviors, and will, when permitted, create a new world in which war, poverty, sickness, and famine will have disappeared.

WE NEED TO CHANGE

You and I cannot instantly change the thought of the world. It is self-evident that we must begin at the only center from which we can operate, and that is within ourselves. There is nothing selfish about this, for as an ever-increasing number of individuals come to understand and apply these principles, just so surely will a new world order come into human experience. We must begin to reconstruct our individual lives. It is for this purpose that we study the Science of Mind. We desire to discover and make use of that subtle creative Power of the Universe which the inspired of the ages have proclaimed to be available to every individual.

The most simple and direct approach which anyone can make to Divine Reality is one of childlike acceptance. This is why the kingdom of God has been likened to a child. The one wishing to demonstrate the creativity of spiritual mind treatment, whether it be for physical healing or in bringing about a betterment of circumstances for himself or others, must become intellectually and emotionally convinced that in such degree as he is aware of his Oneness with God, and in such degree as his thought is in harmony with the Divine Nature, to that degree will his thought be creative of good in his experience. How could it be otherwise if there is but One Mind which we all use?

USING OUR CONVICTIONS

There is a vast difference between announcing a spiritual philosophy and making definite use of a *Universal Principle*. We must not only understand this spiritual philosophy, we must *consciously apply* it to the problems of everyday life. Theory without practice will never accomplish anything worthwhile. The Science of Mind, with its definite technique for spiritual mind treatment, is a statement of principles coupled with a method of practical application. It not only affirms that God, Universal Spirit, is supreme, but it also follows this affirmation with the declaration that the Creative Principle of the Universe is active in human affairs; is doing something for us right now; is creating our experience for us according to the nature of our thought, feeling, imagination, and conviction.

The practical application of this Principle takes place in our own thought. It involves a technique, a certain way of thinking — and this is the crux of the whole matter. The one who gives a spiritual mind treatment feels that he is using a Power which is transcendent of any existing circumstance, that It can make a new condition as easily as It can perpetuate an old one. But, so far as he is concerned, It can create the new condition only in accordance with the pattern of his thought. And because each one of us is an individual we must initiate the new pattern in our experience ourselves. In this way we are coworkers, cocreators with the Infinite.

There is no possible danger which can come from the specific use of the creative power of our thought. It is creative of good in our experience only in such degree as we partake of the nature of infinite Good, which must be harmony, unity, and love. It is well to remind ourselves that the Universe is never violated, and that the *secret place* of the Most High in us is ever accessible. It is impossible to use real spiritual creativity for any purpose which is destructive. The wise man will never make this futile attempt.

WHAT CAN WE EXPERIENCE?

It is a basic concept in the Science of Mind that the idea of good will always destroy an idea of evil, whereas the idea of evil has no power over good. Good remains supreme, unviolated.

Assuming that we desire to give a spiritual mind treatment for a specific thing, for what ends may we feel that we may legitimately pray? The answer seems self-evident. We may use the creativity of our thought for any purpose which increases livingness, joy, constructive self-expression, happiness, peace, and wholeness. Just as light overcomes darkness merely because it is light, so a realization of our unity with good erases negative experiences.

The tools with which we work are thoughts. And our thoughts have a creativity equal to our conviction, and they will always manifest themselves at the level of that conviction, whether we are speaking our word for ourselves or for someone else. And our conviction must include an awareness that we are living in a spiritual Universe, governed by Law — the Law of Mind. Constructive creative thought must, because of its nature, heal any negative condition to which it is specifically directed.

Let us again remind ourselves that no one has ever seen a *principle* in nature, and yet we are always demonstrating that such principles really exist. The one who denies that consciously directed right thought has power is he who is entirely ignorant both of the Universe and Its nature. The only person who can speak with authority is the one who has accepted the Principle of Mind and who has proved It in his own experience. Such a one will never deny Its potency.

WE START WHERE WE ARE

Therefore, never be concerned over what others might say. We need be concerned only with our own attitude toward God, for through the Law of Mind it is only the content of our thought which becomes demonstrated for us. There is a freedom which, in *some degree,* we may prove in our own experience. It is a waste of time to study these ideas and then fail to *make conscious use of them.* Since the only place we can start is within our own thought, we should begin at once to make better use of its creativity. We do not need to wait for a greater understanding; our use of the Law of Mind is the only thing which will increase our knowledge of It.

The Law of Mind is no different from other laws of nature — It exists but we must be aware of It in order to specifically use It. We must feel that our word in a spiritual mind treatment is both cause and effect through the action of this Law; that wherever, whenever, and for whatsoever or whomsoever we speak our word, the living creative Power swings into action, ready, willing, and able to create and to re-create. We must never confuse this with will power or holding thoughts. Spiritual mind treatment is an active, specific presentation of our own thought, of our own inner conviction, to the Law of Mind. The declaration of our word must be so stated as to have a definiteness and a clarity for specific results, and there must be nothing in our minds that contradicts our word.

BUSINESS AIDS

Experience will gradually teach us just what approaches are necessary in individual instances either for ourselves or another. Speaking from the general theory of practice, our treatment should cover whatever seems necessary in an individual case. For instance, if the particular man whom we are treating should say that he cannot succeed because he lacks the opportunity to reveal any qualifications which he may have, it would be necessary to state in treatment that such opportunity does present itself, that he is free to express every creative quality which he possesses. If the one whom we are helping should tell us that there is too much competition in his field, our declaration about him should be so stated as to cover the thought of competition. We might declare that since he is an expression of perfect Spirit, the complete unity of Good in which there is no competition, he experiences no competition. We would not be trying to destroy competition, but rather to eradicate a belief in harmful competition. So far as he is concerned, this is all that would be necessary. This is what we mean by saying that in treatment we must cover whatever seems necessary. Experience alone can teach us to do this, but one will never gain in experience unless he starts.

THE SUPREME TEST

Our whole endeavor is to impart ideas which will enlarge our scope of thinking: To let us discover for ourselves a knowledge which will give us conscious use of the creative power of our thought which we already possess; to place in our hands the tools with which to use this creativity, and to be certain that our understanding is sufficiently clear so that there is no doubt as to our ability to make conscious use of the Science of Mind.

The supreme test in this, as in other things, is in the use we make of it, for we are all some part of a Cosmic Wholeness. The biggest life is the one that includes the most. The more good we set in motion for others the more of that good must come back to us.

CHAPTER VII

WHAT DO YOU EXPECT?

We have been discussing perfect Intelligence, perfect Law, and perfect Life. But a practical question which might arise is: "How much can apparently imperfect man expect to demonstrate?" Should we expect absolute physical perfection, limitless wealth, or flawless happiness?

Of course there must be a sensible and logical answer to such questions. We do not say that because a man thinks *about* a million dollars he will *have* a million dollars. What we do say is this: While it is true that, so far as Principle is concerned, we can have what good we desire according to the Law of Cause and Effect, it is also true that no matter what we may desire we shall only have what we are *able to accept*. Since this accepting is mental, we shall only experience what we are able to embody in our thought. In other words, each one will automatically attract good into his experience in accord with his acceptance of Life. This is one of the principal ideas of the Science of Mind and it is called the Law of Mental Equivalents.

What would fill the needs for one person might not do it for another. What one person might regard as normal, possibly would stagger the imagination of another by its very bigness. Our standard of *expectancy depends entirely upon ourselves*. Every demonstration is made at the exact level of the expectancy, the expectancy embodied in thought. Since no one can step out of or away from himself, it would be impossible for anyone to escape the logic of his own thought.

WHAT IS THE NORMAL STANDARD?

There is a very nice song entitled "Wishing Will Make It So." It sounds encouraging, but it is not true. The world is full of "wishers" who are not "getters." We never get that for which we *merely wish*. A wish means nothing until it becomes a definite declaration that we now possess the good we need, a declaration backed by conviction of the quality and quantity of good which we expect to experience.

At this point we must understand that we have to rise above much of the world's confused thought. The world has dropped its eyes to the ground. Hungry for much, it is satisfied with little. Therefore we must strike out for the heights, away from the mists and fogs of man's doubts, and must see things *through the eyes of Spirit*.

Spirit is the only Reality, but most of man's thinking is colored by the relative. If one has a little better health than his neighbor, he is content. If his business is a little better than the average, he is pleased. If he finds a fuller measure of happiness than that of the general run of mankind, he feels that he is blessed.

He is making the mistake of measuring his experience by an imperfect standard. Instead of establishing his expectancy in accord with the limited experience of mankind generally, he needs to base it on something better and bigger. The standards of the race are always in a state of flux, changing from generation to generation, from day to day, and from individual to individual. But the standard of Spirit is ageless, changeless, unvarying. *It is perfection, nothing less.*

PERFECTION IS THE NORMAL

When the level of the individual's thinking is divorced from that of the world and raised to that of the Spirit, his standard changes from that of imperfection to perfection. And this is the true norm. Regardless of his present experience, man has access to perfection for the minutest detail of his life.

Spirit could not possibly have any idea which is less than perfection. Anything less than this implies an imperfect Spirit, or something opposed to God, which cannot be. Spirit knows only the perfect, and knows nothing of the imperfect. Every step of the great creative activity of Spirit has been characterized by perfection. The tiniest organism adheres to a perfect pattern and functions according to a perfect law.

The blade of grass is a thing of perfection, functioning perfectly in its particular sphere. All its atoms are things of perfection, acting and reacting according to perfect law. This same perfection is true regarding man. But with this exception, man can think and he has gradually built mental concepts of imperfection, has gazed upon them, then has fallen down and worshiped them. Instead of knowing a God of Perfection, man in his imagination has created many gods of imperfection, and they are all creatures of his own imagination — *they have no basis in reality.*

SICKNESS IS ABNORMAL

Perfect health is the thing we should expect — imperfect health is an abnormality. There is no such thing as a miracle in healing. The healing of a cancer is merely an innate perfection asserting itself. But that healing comes *only* where health is regarded as the true, the normal state.

Here we run into the collective thought of man. The past experience of the race has been filled with sickness. We may look around and think, "No one ever has escaped the experience of sickness and hardship." The fact is that only the one who fully expects perfect health is sane. The world says "preposterous" when one declares that health is normal and sickness is subnormal. But he who looks with the eyes of Spirit knows that perfection is the sanest, most natural thing in the universe.

Everyone who ever went against the popular belief had to do it alone. They told Alexander Graham Bell that it was preposterous to imagine that he could send his voice over a wire. They called the steamboat "Fulton's Folly." They sneered at Marconi when he said he could talk without wires (they had accepted Bell by this time), and they have laughed with derision when anyone has dared to stand forth and attempt anything at all which was beyond the realm of their own limited thinking.

So we, in seeking Reality, may go against the accepted beliefs of many if we expect to demonstrate perfection. The mere fact that man has supinely accepted sickness and limitation as necessary does not prove that there is no way out of this misery. For ages man accepted the cold of a fireless world until some intrepid soul struck a spark and started man on his way toward heated homes. Now this is accepted as normal and we wonder how man could possibly have overlooked the greater potential.

WHAT IS THE PERFECTION OF SPIRIT?

Perfection could only be the nature of Spirit. Therefore, the normal in man is the expression in him of what Spirit is. In other words, if man permits Spirit to flow freely in and through him It will manifest those qualities and characteristics which It *is* in Itself.

Man has to consciously find his way back to God. Man is now a thinker let loose in the universe and possessed of research machinery which enables him to observe the handiwork of God and thus to find out more of what God is. There has been no voice from the clouds, no words "written by the finger of God" on stone, no trance revelation to selected individuals. Man has come to know God by observing how God works in the world and in himself. And he has found much. He will undoubtedly find more. But at this time he has discovered enough to lead him out into the bright light of Perfection that exists behind all things. And he needs to follow the intuition of his own soul to discover the living Presence in the universe.

GOD IS LIFE

The universe is full of life and that life is the Life of God, because there is no other source from which it could possibly come. The true norm for man, therefore, is Life — Life abundant — Life to the very fullest extent, unmarred by anything contrary to It. Spirit is eternal, whole, deathless. In fact, Life and death are incongruous, because there is nothing but Life in Spirit, and, therefore, in Its universe. God is Life, and the nearer we come to an understanding of this, and of our Oneness with God, the less we shall be subject to anything that limits Life, which disease certainly does.

The question might be asked, "Why do we talk so much about God?" The answer is both intelligent and logical. We have variously defined God as the Life Principle running through everything, the creative Power in everything, the One Mind or Intelligence at the center of everything. If, instead of the word God one wishes to say Life, Creative Principle, Divine Spirit, Universal Soul, Universal Mind, or just say "It," the same result would be obtained. The principal thing we have to realize is that the Spirit can give us only what we take, and that the taking is mental. Next we must understand that thought patterns become habitual, more or less fixed, although we can always change them. Any mental state that is fixed tends not only to perpetuate itself, but always attracts to itself more which is like itself.

LIFE DOESN'T CHANGE

The thing that we change is not the Reality or the Law of Life, but our own action in It. Its reaction to us will always correspond to our action in It, just as the reflection in a mirror will always correspond to the image held in front of it. Change the image and you will change the reflection. Naturally the more perfect the image, the more perfect will be the reflection.

We all desire certain things. We would like to be happy. Every normal person wishes to be well, and it is not natural for one to desire impoverishment. Surely everyone wishes love and friendship in his life, and all will desire beauty. Does it seem too good to be true that all of these things are really intended for us? Does it seem like an idle daydream to expect this greater good? Rather is it not true that something within us, by some Divine intuition, has already told us that all these things belong to us as a part of our natural inheritance? We have listened so long to the suggestions of imperfection that the song of harmony seems unreal.

PROGRESSIVE THINKING

We must learn to break down the barriers of our limited thinking. Expectancy speeds progress, just as joy and enthusiasm give wings to hope. If one felt that the statements he makes in a spiritual mind treatment were merely repetitions of idle dreams he would indeed be living in a world of fantasy, flying, as it were, from one bough of superstition and vain imagination to another. But in reality there is a deep underlying conviction in every man's mind that life must have a deeper meaning, that goodness must overcome evil, that even death finally must be conquered, and that all that is limiting, all that hurts or that gives pain and suffering, must give way to some Divine Reality. This inner sense is not an illusion; it is not only the guiding star of our hope, it is that without which hope would be impossible.

Just as we have ascertained many of the laws of nature and use them to do our bidding, just as we have harnessed electricity to the wheels of progress and applied it to the comfort of our everyday lives, there is also a Power or a Law which is just as intangible as electricity but which relates to the creative power of our thought, and we may use It. A few great souls have appeared throughout the ages who have understood this. They have been the true saviors of mankind. Moreover, the greatest good which we have ever known has come from their simple teachings.

BELIEVE IN THE UNIVERSE

Every great religion and every great spiritual philosophy has been built on the perception of those who have dared to believe in and trust the Universe. Why should we not do likewise? Why shouldn't we develop the God-Power within us just as we would any other power? Are not our powers God-Powers and should they not be used in a God-like way? The creative power of thought is no exception to this.

It matters not what we have chosen to call it, we are surrounded by a creative Intelligence which responds to our word. Since we may consciously shape our word we may consciously mold our destiny. But we will never do this merely by making a lot of statements about principles, nor even by saying "God is Good." God was Good before we made the statement. The electrical engineer does more than state his principles. He says there is power in the waterfall, there is energy stored in coal and oil and in the wind and the wave. He announces the existence of universal energy. It was there before he proclaimed it. It would still be there if he remained ignorant of its nature. The engineer says that since these energies exist and since we know something of their nature, and since we have discovered how to harness them, why not use them. He tells us that there is a definite technique whereby this energy is converted into power for practical use.

There was a man who lived nearly two thousand years ago who proclaimed a Power and taught that It is ever available to those who believe. Because this Power exists, prayers have been answered, faith has been justified. But someone might say, "You talk so boldly about a vague invisible Principle. Let us weigh and measure It. Let us hold It in our hands and see what It looks like. Let us analyze and dissect It. We refuse to believe in anything which we cannot objectively touch, taste, or handle." What an absurd thought! Who knows how the blush comes to the rose? Did anyone ever weigh and measure the Creative Principle of Life? And yet, does any sane person doubt Its existence?

WHAT WE MUST DO

The great trouble with us is that we haven't yet come to think of the energies of Mind and Spirit in the same natural manner that we think of other energies or laws in nature. Therefore, we have not yet consciously harnessed the Power within us to definite purposes. This is what a student of the Science of Mind must learn to do. This process is never a wistful wishing nor an idle dreaming, it is an intense reality. The Power to live, to create and to expand is already within us — why not use It?

We started this chapter with the assertion that we get, not what we wish for, but what we regard as the normal. And we went on to say that the normal is the expression in us of what Spirit is in Itself. Since Spirit is Life, then we should take time to meditate quietly at this point upon our own inner expectation, and to find out how much of Life we can mentally embody and accept. For this and this alone is what we shall manifest. An imperfect concept of Life means an imperfect experience of It; a perfect concept of Life means a perfect experience of It.

MAN'S GREAT NEED

Truth is that which *is*. God knows nothing which does not exist. Everything that God knows, exists. God does not know limitation. God does not know poverty. God does not know unhappiness. God knows nothing negative *at all*. God knows only that which is positive. It is man alone who has created negative and limiting experiences for himself. So, one should seek to unify himself with God, to look with the eyes of Spirit beyond all appearances, and see Perfection behind all things, to affirm only the Good, knowing that that is what will appear, replacing all unlike Itself.

CHAPTER VIII

YOUR MIND IS A MAGNET

We are always either attracting or repelling. It is impossible to escape this immutable Law of Cause and Effect which governs everything. We are either drawing people to us or repelling them. Our thought is either bringing us happy or unhappy experiences, sickness or health. If we are engaged in business our thought patterns determine whether or not our business is going to be successful, whether it will expand or shrink. How necessary it then becomes for us not to let our thinking be under the domination of our present experiences. This is why a very wise man once told his followers to judge not according to appearances.

We are always attracting the love of others, or their criticism. We are drawing assistance and cooperation into the orbit of our personal experience, or else we are creating frustrations and disappointments. This is because we are always thinking. Mind is the most active thing in the universe. It works ceaselessly, fashioning thoughts into things. Our every thought comes forth in some way as our experience.

We have reached a very happy place indeed, and a desirable stage in our growth, if we no longer give thinking room to negative ideas. Always we should go on to higher levels; always we should be seeking to purify our thought processes. It must have been this idea which led the deep thinker of antiquity to say, "Let the words of my mouth, and the meditation of my heart, be acceptable in thy sight, O Lord . . ." It is our total thought content and belief that creates and maintains the pattern or form for the continuous creative action of Law. The tangible result is manifest in our experience.

BELIEFS PRODUCE RESULTS

Most certainly Jesus laid down a fundamental spiritual law when he told us it is done unto us *as* we believe. How necessary it becomes that we have a solid foundation for our belief. Just what are we going to believe in? This is really what matters. Do we believe that the Universe is for us or against us? Naturally, our beliefs are personal and we all hold individual thoughts about God and the Universe. This is as it should be, but there are certain dominant beliefs which we should entertain, and certain fundamental truths which we should all come to see clearly if we hope to make the most effective use of the Science of Mind.

Surely we should come to believe that the Universe is well disposed toward us, that God is Love, that happiness is our Divine birthright, and that abundance belongs to everyone. Certainly we should believe that the normal state is to be physically well and financially secure.

It is certain that our fundamental beliefs color all of our experiences, whether we are consciously thinking of them or not. Subconsciously our beliefs are always working. It is not at all difficult to decide to change our conscious beliefs; it is easy enough to decide just what good we desire; but if we are going to make practical and effective use of belief, *we must stay with our ideas until they become a part of us.* Belief must be based upon conviction, else we shall only be making believe that we believe. This would be to practice self-deception. We must be sure we have an adequate and logical foundation for our belief, and then we must stay with it.

GOD IN HIS UNIVERSE

We know that the physical universe could not have created itself, for it evidences no power of creativity, motion, or action other than that imposed on it by some force that is nonmaterial. The only nonmaterial force is Consciousness and Its action as intelligent Law. Since the physical universe antedates man by several billions of years, we may be certain that man's thought did not create it. It follows then that at the center and back of the physical universe is Mind. The simplest creature and the tiniest particle of matter are tangible manifestations of the creative activity of Mind. It is in and through the creative Spirit of the universe that man lives and moves and has his being. Not separate from Spirit, but as some part of It, with self-knowingness and consciousness. Man is an individualized center of God-Consciousness, and each individual is unique. No two individuals are alike. And each builds up his individual world of experience as he expresses the Universal Creative Power of Mind within him. What a mystery and how magnificent!

As our thought becomes more God-like we shall have learned to be conscious cocreators with the Divine Creative Principle. It stands to reason that we could not reach this exalted place until we had first learned how to live in harmony with a greater Good. But there is nothing restricting about this since the greater Good also includes our individual good.

What we must learn to do is to exercise the authority which the Universe has invested in us, and create freedom instead of bondage for ourselves. This is done by revising our old order of thought and incorporating a new one. We need not destroy anything in our old thought patterns which was good, we merely drop out the negative and limiting thoughts and expand the good. Thus we pass from the old into the new without confusion.

DON'T BE IRRITATED

When we allow ourselves to become irritated by circumstances we do not like we are only perpetuating such circumstance. On the other hand, when we persist in seeing that which is good, rather than bad, in every person or circumstance, then that which is good is bound to come forth. There is inherent good in all things. Our endeavor to discern this good will enable it to come forth more freely.

We must never close our eyes to the fact that God is in *everything* in His universe, and there is good in everything. But we often have to search for it. When we see only those things which irritate us that is all we shall find. But when we endeavor to find good that is what we attract into our experience.

A proper understanding of this fundamental fact should wipe out any tendency to complain about everything that happens. For if everything, every person and experience, is some action or expression of the All-Good — God — then it follows that we must learn to see some good in all. Otherwise we are reading into things and people something that is not there. In other words, we are seeing only our own misconceptions. And since our thoughts cast their own shadows, we shall actually experience the result of our negative thinking. In this way we confirm our thinking and perpetuate our undesirable experiences.

If, on the contrary, we have grounded ourselves in the fundamental assumption that God is active in a certain situation or person, then we are able to surround it or him with our love instead of our irritation. Very soon *that which we mentally see will come forth.*

Two people are looking at the Grand Canyon. One says, "Wild horses could never drag me back to this place." The other says, "Marvelous! Inspiring! Beautiful! I'm coming back every year." The Canyon is the same, physically, to both. But one's mental reaction is of distaste, the other's of pleasure. In other words, what we read into any experience colors our reaction to it. Therefore, we should try to see God in every man and in every experience. And this means that *we should not allow ourselves to be irritated by anyone,* for we cannot become irritated by God, who is only Good.

THE POWER OF LOVE

Some time ago a young woman came for advice. She worked in an office where the office manager seemed unbearable. She said that she had never seen a man who seemed to take such delight in hurting others. She enumerated the hundred and one petty meannesses he expressed toward her and others. Finally her irritation at him reached a point where she hated the way he held his cigar, disliked every tie he wore, and was irritated by the very tone of his voice.

What had happened was that she had thought only of certain of his *negative* actions until finally his voice, clothes, and everything about him gave her an unpleasant reaction. When it was pointed out to her that she had no responsibility for his actions, only for her own, she began to understand. She began to say to herself, "What rich, full tones are in his voice. That's a beautiful necktie he has on this morning. Doesn't he smile nicely?" She had taken the first correct step which was to *eliminate from her own mind* the irritating qualities with which she was surrounding him. When she was able to go further and say, "He is an expression of Spirit, made of the same spiritual substance of which I am made, striving for happiness just as I am," she was nearer a good result. For it is our *beliefs* that produce the results we experience. Finally she brought herself to say, "How glad I am to be able to work with such a man. I see in him the image and likeness of God. I *steadfastly refuse* to take note of anything less than this."

As a result of her changed attitude the manager changed his attitude, not only toward her but toward others. But this is not the most important thing. That young woman had found *the secret of immunizing herself to irritation,* by coming to the deep-seated *belief* that God pervades the entire universe. She had learned that "if a man say, I love God, and hateth his brother, he is a liar" for the brother whom he sees is merely an expression of God, the Unseen. And in changing her thoughts from irritation to ones of love she was bringing herself into line with the Mind of God, which is only Good.

A PATTERN OF HEALTH

Very frequently when overtaken by sickness we fall into a panic of fear. We must learn to place our faith in good, transposing the thought of fear into one of faith. It will help us to realize that the body is spiritual substance — it is really some part of the Body of God. God pervades it from tip to toe.

In giving a spiritual mind treatment for physical healing one should sense that there is a perfect spiritual pattern of the body. He should try intellectually and emotionally to sense it, just as he senses the atmosphere of harmony. He should know that the spiritual pattern of the body is a reality, otherwise there would be no body. He should know that Life pervades every cell of the body. He should also know that his recognition and realization of the Divine Presence flowing in and through the pattern is what actually heals. It has the power to dissolve *the wrong thought and its negative manifestation,* and to re-establish the pattern of perfection to which we are now giving our full attention.

If one finds himself doubting, he should at once affirm that he *knows* what he believes and that he *believes* what he knows. A spiritual mind treatment is a series of statements made in our minds, an aspect of the One Mind, for ourselves or some other person, or relative to some situation or condition which needs to be changed. The declarations made in Mind are clear-cut statements of our belief and should establish a realization in our own thought that the condition, which ought to be changed, is *now* completely changed. The treatment, to be effective, must arrive at a definite conclusion, and if the treatment is to have any healing power the conclusion at which it arrives must *transcend* the state of consciousness which produced the negative situation.

PRINCIPLE OF GROWTH

We should expect to grow in our understanding and use of constructive thinking and its creative action through the Law of Mind. It is one thing to *say* we believe in this Principle, but it is quite a different thing to *actually* believe in It. Much of our difficulty comes from the conflict between what we think and what we actually believe, deep in consciousness.

If we can hold to the truth that everything in the universe exists for the purpose of aiding us, and never of limiting or hindering us, we will have evolved a faith that can meet all the problems of life. We will have an attitude of relaxation characterized by the word *let*. The opposite attitude we may have had in the past would have been one of forcing things, characterized by the word *must*.

In giving a spiritual mind treatment one should stop when he finds himself tensing and trying to force something to happen. For this "forcing" is an indication that he recognizes the presence of a hostile, opposing power which is arrayed against him, and which he must overcome. This is a belief in duality, the Presence of God and a supposed opposite; good and evil, health and sickness, prosperity and poverty.

There is nothing but God and good in the universe. Good could only contribute to man's growth and development. *Nothing* is ever trying to oppose him. The secret of accomplishment is in "letting" this good come forth. Man's part in the work is to rest in this knowledge, and to *let* Universal Wisdom flow into action. Often a thing may look big to man and lead him into a misguided and tensed sense of "forcing." *Nothing is big or little to Mind.* Man makes things appear large; Spirit knows there is nothing but Itself. When one allows an awareness of Spirit to enter into his pattern of thinking and become his deep belief, he then ceases struggling and "lets" the Divine Perfection and Creativity flow through him into his experience. The one who does this will find that his life is characterized by steadily increasing health, happiness, and prosperity *without any effort on his part* other than choice and conscious direction.

PERSONAL CONFLICTS

Sometimes when a misunderstanding arises between two persons angry words and thoughts follow. When one *knows* that there is only One Mind in the universe, he can relax in the knowledge that there never can be a conflict between expressions of the One Mind. Mind knows nothing but Oneness — Unity. So he endeavors to remove from his own thought any belief that there is an unresolvable difference of opinion. He disregards the *apparent* conflict, and goes back to his fundamental belief: that Mind is One, that his mind and the other person's mind are expressions of that Mind, and that there is a harmonious relationship between the two. He steadfastly refuses to recognize in any way that inharmony is necessary or needs to continue.

Spiritual mind treatment should be built on a sense of Divine Unity and Oneness with Life. When we say that one needs to heal himself of any harsh feeling toward another we are stating something that is very important in treatment. *All healing is self-healing.* The thing which distinguishes the Science of Mind from most psychological methods of approach is right here. In this method the individual treats himself rather than his patient, and yet he treats himself for his patient. What is he really doing? He is trying to convince himself that the person for whom he is working is already both Divine and perfect. He is trying to convince himself that the negative circumstances or situations which he is treating are already filled with Divine and harmonious action. The individual who can convince himself of the idea that he or the one he is helping need not suffer will generally find an immediate physical improvement. It is very important to understand this, since it removes an idea that otherwise might seem to be a barrier or obstacle to one's work. What is this but a more definite understanding of the meaning of those symbolic words: "Ye shall know the truth, and the truth shall make you free."

CHAPTER IX

LIFE CAN BE WONDERFUL

We most certainly do not deny human suffering. What we believe is that although suffering is an experience of the human race there is nothing in the Universe that necessarily makes it so. Naturally we all have had more of it than we desire. But we cannot believe that suffering in any form is a part of the Divine plan, for this would be logically unsound. If we have a suffering God, then man must eternally suffer with Him. This, of course, would be a house divided against itself and is both absurd and unthinkable. In some manner which we do not completely understand we feel that all suffering is a result of ignorance, and we know that the only thing which heals ignorance is knowledge. Knowledge alone can give release.

THE OUTER AND THE INNER

There are two ways of looking at everything. There is an outer and an inner meaning to all life. Jung, in his book, *Psychology and Religion,* tells us that it is impossible to account for anything visible without first understanding that it must have an invisible cause. It stands to reason that every effect must have a cause. If we are starting with the supposition that the Universe is a spiritual system, governed by the Law of Mind, then it follows that discordant thoughts will produce discordant conditions. The outer will always be a reflection of the inner.

Some wise person has said that we shall be subject to suffering so long as we inflict pain on others. This seems like sound philosophy; it is certainly good logic, and it does keep faith with the reasonableness of cause and effect. It is one thing to acknowledge that we have undergone suffering; it is quite another thing to believe that this suffering is imposed upon us by some external force, intelligence, or will. If, on the other hand, we can come to the conclusion that suffering is a result of an ignorant use of the Law of Cause and Effect, then in ascertaining its cause we shall also discover its cure. We get right back to the old, simple but profound proposition that every problem carries its own answer with it.

Generally speaking, whenever the medical profession discovers the cause of any disease it knows how to successfully deal with it. When we discover the mental cause of any particular form of suffering, why shouldn't we consciously change this cause, and, as a logical result of having changed it, reverse the effect? In doing this we would not be destroying the Law of Cause and Effect; we would merely be using It in a different way. If a sense of always having one's feelings hurt seems to produce inflammation in the throat area — which experience seems to verify — then why would it not follow that if we arrive at a place where our feelings are no longer hurt the physical correspondent will also disappear? We will add one more thought to this: So long as we give cause to others for having their feelings hurt, we ourselves are subject to a like sequence of cause and effect.

This places the whole problem where it belongs, for no problem can be solved which is external to consciousness. And if we assume that causes for human problems are beyond our reach, then they are beyond the possibility of change. But if, on the other hand, we assume that the cause of our negative experience must be within the realm of consciousness, then we are not bound by any law as such; we are merely bound by our misuse of it, our ignorance of the way the Law of Cause and Effect operates.

Jesus understood this perfectly when he forgave people their sins, and we have one instance in particular which was outstanding in his experience and teaching. When they brought the man who was born blind to him and asked who sinned, who made the mistake, the man or his parents, Jesus did not argue the problem with them. He took the position that no matter what caused the man's blindness, it could be reversed. In our work we must always take the position that Truth overcomes every apparent obstruction, that we may consciously use an unseen cause to change any manifest effect. We do not believe that there is any cosmic purpose in suffering, or that the Universe is imposing suffering on us to teach us lessons. We believe that *ignorance* alone is the cause of suffering, and enlightenment alone can eliminate it. This is both a sensible attitude and a scientific one.

CAUSE AND EFFECT

There are many negative situations which appear to have their origin in race belief. We are all more or less bound by the sum total of human thought until we individually free ourselves from it.

From a practical viewpoint the Science of Mind views any and all suffering as a logical outcome of mental causes. In seeking relief one should seek to remove the cause so that the effect may also be eliminated. He does not deal with the effect; he deals with the cause, destroys it at its roots, permitting its effect to dry up for lack of nourishment. In actual practice one theoretically resolves things into thoughts and then rearranges his thinking to conform to a basic harmony, taking the position that whenever any circumstance or experience denies a fundamental harmony it is basically wrong. Good is a fundamental reality and all that is contrary to it is a result of the wrong use of the Law of Cause and Effect. We need to build up a consciousness that there is no necessity to suffer, and affirm the presence of our desired good rather than its absence. This rule will prove effective in any and all spiritual mind treatment.

PAIN AS A FRIEND AND TEACHER

Physical pain is not necessarily an enemy, since it calls attention to serious conditions which need to be changed, thus enabling one to take the proper steps in rearranging his life. Therefore we should not be bitter over it nor become melancholy through having experienced it. On the other hand, we must be equally certain that we do not fall under the mistaken idea that illness is imposed upon us by some deific power, as though God were tantalizing us or clubbing us into acquiescence to the Divine will. All experiences should tend to enlarge our awareness of the real purpose of life and help us to arrive at a greater realization of the Spirit that is within us.

A negative condition or limitation is a definite experience, more than imaginary. We cannot consider physical pain or want as being illusions. Primitive religion taught a dualistic view of the Universe, that there were two opposing powers — God and the devil, or Good and evil. We can trace this belief back through our own Christian theology to that of the Hebrews, Persians, and Babylonians. But merely because millions of people have believed in the necessity of evil, or that evil is imposed upon us by some outside source, we need not accept their verdict. The fact that many persons have believed a thing to be true will not make it true. We view evil, lack, want, limitation, sickness, pain, and human suffering as real experiences; but, nevertheless, a denial of the Life-Principle Itself, which is only Good.

PROVING OUR POSITION

There is only one way for us to prove that this is a correct position and that is to put this philosophy to the test of actual experience. Suppose, for instance, we lack friends. We have no friends, see no friends, believe in no friends, therefore we feel isolated from the rest of humanity. It might be a little difficult at first to realize that the cause is in our own mind. As a matter of fact, it wouldn't help merely to recognize this. We must learn to reverse our pattern of thinking relative to friendship. We must *become* friendly, in both thought and action.

In actual practice we mentally encompass friendship everywhere we go, believe that everyone we meet will be friendly, expect happy human relationships. We must go even further than this and make the definite declaration that friendship is a law of our life now active in our own individual experience. Gradually, as we reverse our inner negative thought processes, we shall find a change coming in our external world. People will become friendly. We will be invited to group gatherings, others will include us in their circle of friends, and finally we shall discover ourselves to be centers through which love and friendship flow out from us and come back again into our own experience.

GOOD AND EVIL

Our ideas of good and evil are more or less relative. As we awake to the fact that certain things do not work out well, we seek a greater good and we call the lesser good, evil. In the dim ages of antiquity the ancestors of man lived by the law of strength. They killed each other without any qualms of conscience. But slowly, as the race evolved, men became dimly aware of stirrings within them that proclaimed man's Divinity, and gradually a new standard was established. Until that time there was no consciousness of sin and man had no sense of guilt. As man developed and advanced the more perfect standard emerged, and time made "ancient good uncouth."

If we were to carry this proposition to its ultimate conclusion we should see that somewhere along the line of one's evolution he will arrive at a place where it will be impossible for him to wish harm to others. When that time comes it will be equally impossible for harm to be imposed upon him. This new vision is not so much a theological mandate, or a philosophical conception, as it is a matter of awakening to the greater Good. It is something which comes from the stirrings of the Divine Spirit within us.

NEGATIVE DESIRES

In the new psychological outlook on alcoholism, for instance, the patient is not taught so much to resist the desire as he is taught to envision a new life, in which his desire to drink plays no important part whatsoever. The habit thus dies for lack of nourishment.

In spiritual mind healing we deal with such a case by knowing that man's spirit, being some part of the Spirit of God, is entirely free from any and all harmful desires, is happy and satisfied within itself, and is complete and perfect within itself. That there is a natural stimulation of Spirit in and through him and the urge for self-expression finds a natural healthy outlet in constructive action. The energies of the old habit are transmuted into a new and joyous form of self-expression. This new self-expression is so much more complete that the old is entirely obliterated by it. The old habit has ceased to function.

This is a good example of how it is that spiritual mind treatment does not use will power, but rather a willingness. This is neither mental coercion nor compulsion. It is an acceptance of the creative Law of Good within us. It is really the uncovering of the Divine at the center of our being. Goodness and badness are merely different levels of experience, and we ever have the right to choose the best.

WE ARE BORN FREE

We believe that back of all experiences of living there is a spiritual Reality which, if properly adhered to, causes everything to work out rightly. When in our ignorance we think negatively the Law of Mind must, of necessity, produce a negative experience for us. The attendant experiencing of pain, lack, or inharmony warns us that we are on the wrong track and we begin to inquire why. For every problem which confronts us we set up a "Why?" and are never satisfied until the problem is solved. Somehow or other we instinctively know that we are born to be free, and we may always turn to that Reality which can and will make everything right for us.

Moses said that he set before his followers a blessing or a curse, "A blessing, if ye obey the commandments . . . a curse, if ye will not obey the commandments . . ." When we think in a negative way we suffer; when we think in a positive way for good we are automatically released from suffering. This brings us to the fundamental proposition that there is One Power in the universe, but there are two ways of using It.

Most of us learn through experience. Perhaps as we grow our awareness of Reality will become so deepened that undesirable experiences will be mostly eliminated. There seems no time set as to when this shall occur for we each set the time ourselves. One thing is certain: While we would give pain, we shall receive it; while we are the cause of hurt, we shall be hurt.

LIFE IS FOR US

The Universe Itself is foolproof, and somewhere along the line each one of us will have to learn that Love is a principle of Nature – a "love so limitless, deep and broad, that men have renamed it and called it God." Suppose we start, then, with the proposition that Life desires only our good, that fundamentally It is for us and never against us. And suppose we add to this proposition the idea that what the Creative Principle does for us It must do through us. Shall we not, of necessity, arrive at the conclusion that our whole pattern of thought should be changed to comply with this new concept?

Generally speaking, such a change in our way of thinking is not brought about in a moment's time. It does not follow, however, that since it is not brought about in a moment life should remain a continual struggle. Suppose we take the happier viewpoint and become willing to gradually change our mental outlook. In actual practice we should take a few moments every day in meditation to realize our freedom, to sense that we are surrounded by an eternal Goodness, and in our minds to picture our lives as more nearly ideal.

After we have firmly established in thought this new concept of ourselves, we should declare that it is now the law in our experience. We should affirm that we are surrounded by an infinite Intelligence which directs us and an infinite Power which propels us and an infinite Goodness whose whole desire is that we shall experience a complete livingness, a perfect joy. As we set this scene on our mental stage we should also realize that we must become the actor in it. We must inwardly think and outwardly act as though this idea were real. Then it will become real.

At first this may be difficult. But as we more and more realize that constructive thinking is bringing greater good into our experience, we shall more completely come to see that we are dealing with absolute and immutable Law. Then we shall no longer set any limit to the good which we are to experience. Having realized that good belongs to the Universe Itself, we shall seek to embody it. We shall enter into the greatest partnership in life — our partnership with God. And in the close intimacy of this conscious contact with Reality we shall come to sense a Divine Presence overshadowing and indwelling us. We shall no longer feel lost, but will have found our real Self. Then every experience in life will be good.

CHAPTER X

USING THE LAW OF MIND

Spirit is the only *conscious* Intelligence in the universe. Because of this, It is the only *directive* Intelligence in the universe. Man's conscious mind, being part of the Mind of Spirit, is likewise directive. Thus man can mold the conditions in which he chooses to live.

The mind of man is some part of the Mind of God, therefore it contains within itself unlimited possibility for expansion and self-expression. The conscious mind of man is self-knowing. It can know and recognize man's true self. It can range the entire universe to assemble knowledge and facts. It can take facts, evaluate them, balance them, arrive at conclusions. This ability to choose between evidences, and to accept or reject them, is the result of man's conscious ability to think independently of conditions.

The Divine Self-Knowingness in man sets him apart from all creation. It is this which enables him to work out his own destiny according to a definite Law of Cause and Effect. For his choosing and directive mind enables him to make his choices, and his "accepting" of his choice enables it to become manifest in the environmental side of life through the action of Law. There is only One Mind, One Law, One Creation — the Mind, Law, and Creation of God. God and man are One in all three aspects of expression.

EVERYTHING ARISES FROM MIND

In Universal Mind is contained everything that ever was, is, or shall be. That is, everything is there *in essence*. This is difficult for us to grasp, because our senses tell us that things originate in different ways, or through different creative processes. Until one sees clearly that Mind is the *only creative agency* in the universe, he is going to be puzzled by apparent incongruities in his study and practice. When he realizes that all other *apparent* creative agencies are merely Mind working in different ways, he will see the singular unity running through every activity and every manifestation of Power in the universe. When he grasps the truth that things exist in the Universal Mind as ideas, and that *ideas take form and become things* as the result of the action of Mind within and upon Itself, he is getting nearer to an understanding of the entire creative process.

In Mind is the invisible essence of all substance, unformed as pure energy. This energy exists everywhere throughout the universe, waiting to take form. It takes form as man makes his demand upon himself — that is, Spirit in man is making Its demand upon Mind in man to take tangible form. The essence of substance, while ever ready to take form, is unable to do so because it lacks self-knowingness. Man as spirit possesses self-knowingness, therefore when he makes his demand Mind flows into form as substance, and the creation or demonstration is made.

All of this may seem very abstract and far removed from the settlement of daily problems. On the contrary, it is the most practical and intimate knowledge possible, and is fundamentally necessary to clear thinking. In the limitless nature of Mind exists everything that we shall ever experience, even though right now it may lie there in an unformed state. It can flow out into form *only under the directive word* of God and of man; God in the Universe; man in his little world. Thus when man speaks, his word is creative.

Mind in Its unformed state, containing the potential of *everything* that man ever hopes to accomplish or have, can be called forth into individual use. The entire resources of the Universe are at man's call. So, in man's little world he gets nothing except that which he has first formed as a mental concept or idea. Every dollar he ever makes, every joy he ever experiences, every surge of health he ever enjoys, the home he is to own, the business he is to build, all, all exist *now* in Mind, awaiting his mental formulation of them *within his own consciousness*. Every bit of business we ever do, every condition of health, *must* come out of consciousness, for our mind is some part of the One Creative Mind. Both body and supply are plastic. They are thoughts maintained in form. One should never lose sight of the fact of the plastic, spiritual nature of everything he ever touches. It is fluidic in its origin, concrete in its manifestation. Without our recognition of its original plasticity there can never be an intelligent calling of it into form. Ponder this deeply — it will repay you again and again.

THE GIANT WITHIN

Man's mind is limitless because it is the Universal Mind individualized. As an individualization of Universal Mind man's mind contacts the Law of the Universe and thus makes use of the creative factor in him. It is a tremendous Power which man is thus authorized to use. This knowledge is staggering in its implications.

The Law of Mind, being a law of reflection, can only respond by corresponding, by making our experiences correspond to our thoughts. Thus man, as a result of his pattern of thinking or spiritual mind treatment, may receive only and exactly that which he is able mentally to embody. *Things are thoughts clothed in substance*. A tiny mental acceptance makes for a tiny demonstration, through the law of correspondence. A large acceptance makes for a large demonstration. In other words, we hold up our mental concepts before the mirror of creative Law, which has no choice but to reflect them back to us as our experience, but still our thought — thought in form. Of course there is nothing large and small to the action of Law which creates everything.

The Law of Mind, the giant within and around us, is always creating for us. But what *specific* direction are we giving It? Our every thought is a directive! Fulfillment of man's thought is Its nature. And as man awakes to this fact he then will make better use of his thought. We should use the Law definitely, specifically, and *with a conscious knowledge that we are using and directing It*. In this way man's conscious thought has power, and may be creative of good in his experience.

THE CORNERSTONE OF TREATMENT

We should seek to develop an emotional as well as an intellectual conviction in our spiritual mind treatments. Our mental acceptancés of good should be filled with conviction, warmth and color. These are properties of the emotions and can be cultivated. The Law responds to emotional conviction more quickly than to any other mental attitude.

A beginner in the study of the Science of Mind should first master the intellectual phases of the subject. He should get his facts straight. He must understand the principles underlying his philosophy and the foundations on which they rest. His knowledge and understanding should be on solid ground, with no lingering doubts. But all of this will be of but little avail unless he also embodies a *feeling,* senses a warm intimacy with Spirit. It is not enough just to have a cold intellectual grasp of truth. There should be a deep inner conviction of God as Presence in and about us, and the limitless availability of good.

There must be a blending of our entire being in spiritual mind treatment. The emotions and the intellect must not be in conflict with each other but always united, single in content and intent. This brings a feeling of reality into our work. Quite naturally, *feeling* can develop and grow just as the intellect. Each demonstration makes feeling grow and intensify, for we become more and more convinced that Law is responding to us and that we are coworkers with Spirit.

The person who spends fifteen minutes a day in meditation on these things, and the remainder of the time in careless thinking, is not very likely to develop this valuable quality of *feeling* which makes the difference between understanding treatment and making it work. A growth of feeling can develop as a result of considering the action of Law and Life about us. Consider the way Law performs Its wonders within the human body, keeping aware of the marvel of digestion, of elimination, of taste, of appetite, of the various cravings or hungers, or the intricate workings of the brain and nerves. When one is aware of these things it means that there is an inner conviction of the intricate nature of the laws of Life and an accompanying faith that there is an Intelligence behind them. This leads into the *feeling* we have been speaking about.

The marvels of the heavens are awe-inspiring, as well as the mystery of life as seen in plants, fruits, and flowers — their germination, budding, growth, and reproduction. All of these things are beyond man's power to duplicate. They are rich sources of that deep inner conviction that lends "feeling" to his treatment.

A hive of bees or a colony of ants can arouse a sense of wonder. Bird life, the mother instinct, and the marvels of instinctive life in all kinds of animals, the wonders of chemistry, the atomic world, the voice of man and his ability to communicate thought by means of it — these and thousands of other things give evidence of the infinite creativity of Nature open to his thought. We need to take the time in meditation for an appreciation and a reverence for all life, imbuing our thoughts with a feeling of adoration for all that Life is.

It may be a matter of surprise for some to note the way in which thoughts enrich themselves when they are focused on a specific subject. A column in the newspaper, a word on the radio or television, a conversation in a drawing room, an advertisement on a billboard, any one may bring into one's consciousness the very idea that clarifies the whole matter. While the mind is closed to knowledge these things fall unheeded upon our eyes or ears, but when we are "alive" to them they jump out at us from the most unexpected places. Thus we free our thought from our limitations. The unfettered mind is that rarity which the world needs so much these days.

CLEAR THINKING VERSUS DAYDREAMING

We should be very careful to distinguish between daydreaming and creative treatment. While the preceding suggestions are valuable in that they build up a body of thought upon the various activities of the One Mind, they are not mental treatments. Mental treatment is a series of definite declarations for something particular and specific which we wish to experience. A period of meditation is splendid for forming the background of a treatment, but the concrete results are produced by the exact activities known as "treatment."

During treatment we do not wish, we *know*. We do not dream, we *state*. We do not hope, we *accept*. We do not beg, we *announce*. We definitely determine the nature of the good we desire, declare it specifically, accept it as our experience now, knowing that it will be manifested in accord with Law. If we need five hundred dollars we would not speak our word for "some money." We make it specific that we have an *abundance out of which our need is fulfilled*.

NOT FORCE, BUT "LETTING"

We should learn to think clearly and to allow our thought patterns to be consistent. We must always remember that we do not *make* our thought creative. It is just its nature to be creative; we think, we relax and allow our thoughts to be productive. With confidence and conviction we know that through Universal Mind we have immediate acccess to the limitless Power and Energy of the Universe Itself.

We also distinguish between "holding thoughts" and holding things in thought. One is an attempt at an impossible coercion; the other is a mental acceptance. We frequently need to come back again and again to this point, for we will often find that a tendency to force issues creeps in. One can tell when his attitude is incorrect by a feeling of strain. Always remember that there is no sense of strain in a good mental treatment. To *hold* thoughts, through the exercise of will power, as though we were pouring our mental power into the things, does no good because it uses but a tiny fraction of the power at our disposal. On the other hand, "to hold an idea in thought" as though we were *letting* something happen, is to use the greatest power of all. Our thought is as a container which God alone can fill to overflowing.

If at any time we find ourselves doubting our ability to think specifically, we should let the immediate problem go. Then we should look to our own inner life, taking the necessary time to regain the consciousness that it is not I, "but the Father that dwelleth in me, he doeth the works." We must treat ourselves until we do believe, for it is the inner mental *and* emotional acceptance that is the key to successful treating, not the sweat and toil of our individual process of thinking.

Remember that Spirit exists, always, at the center of all form. It is forever expressing in and as tangible form. The forms of Its expression may come and go, but It is changeless and eternal. We personally have form but we are still some part of Spirit. Since Spirit is at the center of everything and in Its action as Law always responds to our thought, there is no limit to Its creativity for us *except the limitations which we ourselves impose on our experience of It.*

CHAPTER XI

SUGGESTIONS FOR EFFECTIVE PRAYER

We definitely believe that there is a very great efficacy in prayer. But we need to clarify just what we mean by prayer. It means many things to many people. Our idea of prayer is based on the fact that there is a supreme Intelligence, God, Mind, or Consciousness that is ultimate Reality, which is both the source of and is all things. The physical world as we know it is the word or thought of God become manifest. And the manner in which the "word" becomes tangible is through the orderly process of Law; another way of saying God acts in an orderly and consistent fashion.

From this foundation we have discovered that our own minds are individual expressions of the One Mind, and that, as a result of this, our words or thoughts are similarly creative. They are specific causes and their equivalent results manifest in and as our experience. We have nothing to do with whether they are creative or not, it is their nature to be so because of the fact they spring from the activity of the One Mind individualized as our minds.

We are not caught in a universe controlled by a blind force. We are in the midst of and part of an intelligent, continually creative, dynamic *conscious* activity. God is ever going forth into new expression; and every word we speak, every thought we think is a further creative activity of God at the level of our expression of God.

WHAT CAN WE PRAY FOR?

We are definitely opposed to the idea of prayer as a series of pleadings to a capricious God who might or might not grant us our desires. This old idea was coupled with a sort of moral policing which taught that certain things militated against the possibility of receiving answers to prayer and were generally frowned upon in theological circles. Some of them were fairly harmless, such as card playing, theater going, and dancing, and others included habits such as liquor and tobacco.

We believe that the individual is the best judge of the desirability of such things. But if one finds that any personal habit or practice clouds his vision of Reality it should be dropped from his life, because anything that hinders one from constructive thinking will to the same degree hinder a complete manifestation of the good he desires. This is a matter of personal growth and not in any way connected with a Divine policeman.

We do not believe in praying for a thing and using the argument that we will use it for a good purpose if we get it. The Law knows only to create according to our mental equivalent of the good we desire, and It will not work any more swiftly because we want to do good with the answer.

We do not believe in praying for something "because we are in such want and must have it." It is true, we pray for things we must have, but the world is full of people who want and need things and who never get them because they have never built up the proper mental equivalent, a conscious belief in them.

We *do* pray with a quiet, calm, assured confidence that we can have *anything* that we can mentally accept. That the Law immediately swings into action to the end that It will create for us that which we believe and have faith in. We do not pray with the proviso, "Give us this if it is God's will for us to have it," for we believe that since it is God's Nature to express Himself, it must be His Nature to give us anything that contributes to our growth, happiness, and achievement without being harmful to someone else.

FUNDAMENTAL HARMONY OF THE UNIVERSE

There is a fundamental harmony in the Universe. Mind creates for us out of Its limitless reservoir of unformed spiritual energy or essence. It never has to take from anyone because It has unlimited raw material upon which to draw. Therefore, it is not necessary for our brother to be made poor so that we can have his substance with which to become rich. There is plenty to make both of us rich and satisfied.

But if we feel our happiness may only be gained by impoverishing another we must in all wisdom forego any desire to have that thing. If we should persist in trying to get it, by the same Law whereby we would get it we would lose it. For if we cause our brother's tears to flow, then, by that same action, our tears will be made to flow. If we bring sorrow into the life of another, then into our lives shall sorrow be brought.

No one should desire a good that he does not want for others. That which he wishes for himself he must wish for all others, because all are expressions of the One God. Everywhere, recognizing the fundamental harmony of the Universe and the universal brotherhood of man, we "rejoice with them that do rejoice."

PRAYER IS ACCEPTING, NOT PLEADING

Effective prayer, based upon a faith that is logical and scientific, is an *attitude of mind which is so convinced of its own idea—which so completely accepts it—that any contradiction is unthinkable and impossible.* We should memorize this definition.

Our faith is based upon the conviction that infinite Mind has all Intelligence, all Ability, all Power, all Wisdom, and knows how to create anything. We can think of the most difficult thing it is possible for our finite minds to imagine, and can rest in the assurance that Mind knows how to solve the problem or to create the new condition. Our faith is likewise based upon the fact that the Universe is a system of Law and Order, and that the Law of Mind always responds according to the nature of our thought. The Law never reasons with us, saying, "You know, I don't think that would be a good thing for you to have." We have faith in the undeviating neutrality of the Law. It has no preferences. It never draws back and says, "That goes against the grain with me." It is absolutely neutral. If It could talk to us It would say, "You go ahead and name it, and I'll make it." It does not like to make one kind of thing more than another. It is willing to create whatever we dictate through our pattern of thought. The Law is an intangible principle of Mind that operates in this unswerving, obedient way because it is Its nature to do so.

We are able to consciously avail ourselves of the action of the Law when we recognize Its nature. When we understand that the mind in man is an individualization of the Mind of God — Spirit — then we know when we speak our word of Good that it is the word of Spirit which is being spoken, which is the Law of its own fulfillment. We rise far above the idea of puny man standing erect and calling upon the great Creative Mind to do his bidding. For when man speaks his word, being the expression of God, that word becomes the word of God and is manifest. Thus we can see why we release our thought, word, or prayer. We do not keep clinging to it. God "said" and it was done. As man speaks as Spirit, if his mental acceptance is on the level of his word, it is done.

EXACTNESS IN SPIRITUAL MIND TREATMENT

A spiritual mind treatment must include within itself *everything* that we want the answer to contain. We must remember that the Law does not reason. It does not put in extra things that we forgot, or take out things that we did not notice were harmful. It takes *exactly* what we put in our treatment, and this alone is what It creates. Some time ago a woman who all her life had wanted a home with beautiful grounds came into a California city and treated that she would demonstrate just such a home. Within two months she found exactly what she wanted, at a bargain price: fourteen rooms, acres of ground in lawn, flowers, and fruit trees; rambling old stables with servants' quarters above them, and all in the most delightful setting.

But she had never thought of putting into her treatment the idea of sufficient income to take care of all this. The water bill alone was sufficient to stagger her. And before many months she gave up the effort and moved out. The Law of Mind acts specifically on what we include in our treatment, no more and no less.

A woman had a bookstore. Few people came in. She decided to pray for more activity. She prayed along this line: She built up a mental picture of crowds of people coming in and out of her store. The crowds came, but she had omitted to include the idea that those who would come would appreciate her goods, want to buy them, have the money to buy them, and would buy them. The crowds handled her books, which became shopworn and their value decreased. She was in despair until she realized that the Law was giving her just what she had asked for — activity. Then she added these other ideas to her treatment. The result? Good crowds, good business, and good financial returns.

TREATING OTHERS

When we give a spiritual mind treatment we have a definite intention in our thought. Our treatment is given for a specific purpose. Let us assume that it is for someone's physical healing. We become quiet within our thought and reassure ourselves of the reality of the infinite Power with which we are dealing, erecting an altar of faith and conviction in the sanctuary of our own consciousness. Then we declare that our word is for the person whom we are treating. This directs our treatment *for him* rather than for someone else. All treatment should have *conscious direction* and *definite intention*. Next we make a series of statements, which should automatically flow out of our conviction since there is no magic in words themselves. The statements used should not be stereotyped, but should flow spontaneously from our awareness of the Perfection of God now manifesting in that person.

If we wish to give a spiritual mind treatment for an increased activity in someone's affairs, our statement must be so formulated as to convince ourselves of that activity. What we really are doing is creating an idea of activity for someone; we are not trying mentally to convince him of anything, we are only *convincing ourselves of an idea about him.* Therefore we are freed from any burden of thought as to whether or not he is receiving the treatment. Our whole endeavor is to convince ourselves about the other person, to assure ourselves that there is a Divine activity in his affairs, that this activity is functioning in everything he does; it is surrounding him with love and friendship; it goes before him and prepares his way; it opens the doorway of opportunity to him; it compels him to make right judgments, to act intelligently; it inspires both his thought and his act. Everything that he does prospers. Spirit enlightens his mind and gives enthusiastic buoyancy to his acts. We might also state, if it seems necessary, that our word removes all doubt, fear, and uncertainty.

ANSWER TO PRAYER IS IN THE PRAYER ITSELF

When a prayer or treatment is released it is a completed thing. It is then in the hands of the Law and will be carried forward into manifestation, just as it is. The person who speaks his word, releases it, but is filled with doubt and misgiving as to whether it will ever be fulfilled, has his answer right then. That prayer will be answered, but in reverse. *All prayers are answered,* although not always in the way we would like. But they are answered *according to the individual's pattern of thinking and conviction at the time.*

If our prayers are released, as Jesus' were, with the fullest confidence that the Law can do nothing else but answer them, our demonstrations will come thick and fast. If they are released with only partial acceptance, then they will be only partially answered. If with little or no inward conviction, then the answers will be of a like nature. There is no escape from this, and no exception. Remember, we are dealing with inexorable Law, which never deviates and never varies. *It knows only to obey.*

The Law of Mind is impersonal, like the law of electricity which will move into action for anyone who observes the principles governing its flow. An Einstein or an ignorant Hottentot may press the button. The electricity does not care who it is, for it is its nature to flow at the touch of that button. The tiny fingers of a three-year-old child may set it into action. There is only one prerequisite — the button making the connection *must* be pushed. The Law of Mind will always flow in the direction of constructive creative activity when we understand and apply the principles by which It works. We have the mightiest force in all the world to command. We can step out of a prison of ignorance and fear, and into the light of a constructive expectancy which will remake our world for us.

THE ATTITUDE OF REJOICING

In releasing our word to the action of the Law we do so with a glad and thankful heart. Giving thanks is a further indication that we have fully released our word. It means that we are sure of the completion of the creative process; that there are no lingering doubts. The person who is still unconvinced does not rejoice — he waits until he sees if it is going to work. But if one has done his work thoroughly and well, he can turn his back upon that particular spiritual mind treatment, give thanks for its certainty, and rejoice in its fulfillment, even though he has not seen it outwardly fulfilled as yet.

CONCLUSION

We have come a long way, encountered a variety of ideas and subjects. The meaning of them, the value of them, and their practical application in the matter-of-fact business of everyday living is all that counts.

At some time or other all theories, all books, all teachings have to be literally thrown aside. We have to become quiet and, in the solitude of our own thought, discover for ourselves what it is we actually believe; and then proceed to put that faith into creative action through patterns of thinking built around that faith.

Theories are fine but meaningless except for idle speculation unless we practically apply them to any and all problems and situations which may confront us. It is wonderful to say we believe in prayer, but what can it mean to us unless we pray? There comes a time in the process of our own growth and development when we have learned enough and we must start using what we have learned. Otherwise we can find ourselves spending a lifetime gathering together ideas which will be just a mass of interesting information of no practical value.

Regardless of how little or how much we may feel we have learned about the Science of Mind and spiritual mind treatment, the only time to start to make use of it is *now*. We have to start using today whatever it is we may know or we shall find that the time never does come when we feel we know enough.

The real secret to the practical application of the Science of Mind lies not in how much we know, but in the application of what we do know. And the application means only that we have to apply it, not just think about applying it.

The results, large or small, much or little, depend entirely on the degree of conscientious endeavor, enthusiasm and joy, conviction and faith we can bring to bear on any particular situation.

No one else can do any of this for us. We alone must do the applying for the Science of Mind to be a practical dynamic factor in everyday living. It's up to us.